THE

Martin Gostelow

CONTENTS

rich bird life

unspoiled nature

ALONG THE DANUBE

Who can hear the name Danube without thinking of that most famous of Strauss waltzes: "On the Beautiful Blue Danube"? Beautiful it certainly is, but in reality it's more a brownish yellow than blue, due to the lime and mud stirred up from the river bed. The Danube's romance lies in the medieval castles, baroque churches and rococo palaces it passes on its way through central Europe and the Balkans, as well as the historic cities that have grown up along its banks.

International River

The great waterway begins in southwest Germany at the confluence of the Brege and the Brigach in Donaueschingen, and flows through eight other countries to the sea: Austria, Slovakia, Hungary, Croatia, Serbia, Romania, Bulgaria and Ukraine. Over a stretch of just 570 m, the Danube also flows through Moldova, making it another member of the International Danube Commission. Its 2,860 km (1,770 miles) make it Europe's second longest river, after the Volga. Barge traffic starts at the cathedral town of Ulm, larger vessels at Kelheim. Today, completion of the Main-Danube Canal, also called Europa Canal, extends navigation from the North Sea to the Black Sea in Southeastern Europe.

Through Austria and Hungary

The Danube crosses from Germany into Austria at Passau, established as a frontier town by the Romans. It flows through the major port town of Linz to the Habsburgs' grand imperial city of Vienna. From Slovakia's capital, Bratislava, the river follows the Hungarian border until it makes a dramatic 90-degree turn at the Danube Bend and heads south to the Hungarian capital of Budapest. Here, it cleaves through the city, separating the old hill town of Buda from the more modern and much flatter Pest. Beyond the suburbs, the river returns to its bucolic mood, flowing through flat and fertile countryside. In all, the Danube's passage through Hungary stretches for 417 km (260 miles).

Danube Confederation

From Budapest to the Black Sea, the river has regularly acted as a natural border. Roman sentries and Dacian warriors kept watch on each other across the lower Danube; centuries later the armies of the Habsburgs faced the Ottoman Turks. Many of the towns were founded in Roman times, and medieval fortresses and castle ruins still attest to the battles which were fought here. Under the Austro-Hungarian Monarchy (1683–1918), the countries on the middle and lower reaches seemed to be united—the first and only time that a "Confederation of the Danube" has been a reality.

What's in a Name? The Donau in Germany and Austria, Duna in Hungary, Dunav to the Serbs, the Croats and the Bulgarians, Dunaj in Slovakia and Dunărea in Romania, the Danube was known as Istros to the ancient Greeks—and is Tuna to the Turks. The name derived from the Latin Danubius, the name of a Roman river god. However, its roots are far older, either from the Celtic or perhaps the Farsi *Danu*, meaning quite simply "to flow" or "to run". This ancient term is at the base of several other European rivers—the Donetsk, the Dniepr, the Don in Russia, and also the English River Don.

Tributaries

On its way to the Black Sea, the Danube passes through a succession of incredibly varied landscapes. In the Great Hungarian Plain (Nagy Alföld) it is joined by major tributaries: the Drava, the Tisza and the Sava. In those sections of the Danube with a very slight drop, such as along the Slovak-Hungarian border, in southern Hungary and northern Croatia, flood-plains are inundated year after year. The flooding has produced a remarkable zone of woods, ponds and streams, now protected as nature reserves and national parks, offering a refuge for richly diversified wildlife.

Iron Gate

The Danube achieves its greatest breadth below Belgrade. Further south, spectacular scenery awaits the voyager, as the river carves a cleft through the Southern Carpathian Mountains at the narrow gorge of the Iron Gate. A hydroelectric power plant was built here in 1971, making a major impact on the natural environment, but at least one positive result was that this stretch of the river, previously feared for its "cataracts", became navigable for ships.

From the Iron Gate, the river flows into the lowlands of Walachia, where it is hemmed in on the Bulgarian side by craggy mountain spurs, whilst the opposite, Romanian bank is flat and marshy. The Danube turns northward before reaching the Dobrogea tableland, to turn back eastward at Galaţi, a large port town in eastern Romania. After this final dogleg, the marshy delta region begins.

The People

The Danubian region is a mosaic of diverse peoples. Today's Romanians are proud to claim Dacians and Romans as their ancestors; those of the Bulgarians were Slavs and Thracians. Germans, too, have had an impact on the culture of the region: in the 12th century, King Géza of Hungary brought Saxons into Transylvania, and in the 18th century Archduchess Maria Theresa of Austria settled Swabians (or Schwaben) on the lower Danube to revitalize and cultivate deserted lands.

The political upheavals of the 20th century forced the majority of the descendants of these settlers to return to their former homeland.

The symbolic source of the Danube in the castle park of Donaueschingen. | A painterly view of Stein on the Danube bank. | The imposing Chain Bridge in Budapest. | Waterlilies in bloom.

Huber/Schmid

istockphoto.com/ene

istockphoto.com/Rus

Conversing on a quiet riverbank in Passau, the "City of Three Rivers".

Jean-Paul Minder

FLASHBACK

About 250,000 years ago, *Homo palaeohungaricus*, a primitive form of human being, settled in the middle Danube valley, now Hungary, attracted by the abundance of water and wildlife, and perhaps even by the hot springs that remain a magnet to this day.

The First Residents

Trade along the Danube developed as far back as the Neolithic period (ca. 6000 BC). The Thracians, the original inhabitants of what is now Bulgaria, spread to the lands between the lower Danube and the northern Aegean around 1000 BC. By the 7th century BC, Greek sailors reached the Danube delta and explored, opening the way for commerce.

Celtic tribes established themselves in the valley of the upper Danube, now southern Germany, by 600 BC. They spread eastwards, settling along the middle Danube and its tributary the Sava, and in the 3rd century BC built a fortress on the site of the future Belgrade. Under pressure from the Romans, Germanic tribes from northern Europe and the Iranian-descended Sarmatians, Celtic domination was broken by around 120 BC. In present-day Romania, the Dacian kingdom was born.

Rome Moves In

From 27 BC, under Emperor Augustus, the Romans' conquest of the Danube valley made the river they called the Danubius (and in its lower reaches, the Ister) the empire's northern border. On the other side lived a variety of tribal peoples the Romans labelled barbarians, among them Celts, Pannonians and Illyrians. A line of fortifications (Limes) was built along the river to repel barbarian incursions. Some 20,000 Roman soldiers were deployed between Vienna and Budapest, and still more along the upper and lower reaches of the river. A Roman fleet patrolled its waters and strongholds were constructed at strategic points on its banks. These quickly grew into flourishing towns, including Castra Regina (Regensburg), Vindobona (Vienna), Aquincum (Budapest), Singidunum (Belgrade) and Sexantaprista (Ruse). Other important riverside fortresses such as

Ratiaria (Vidin) and Nicopolis ad Istrum (Nikopol) were built at the mouths of tributaries.

In AD 106, the expansionist Emperor Trajan defeated the Dacians and so gained control of the entire course of the Danube, as well as extensive lands to the north, roughly the area now covered by Romania and Moldova. His successor Hadrian called a halt to further conquest, in order to concentrate on organizing and defending the vast territories under Roman rule.

In the 3rd century, Goths hailing from north of the Black Sea penetrated southwards to the Danube and crossed it in force. It took a strong Roman army led by the Emperor Gallienus and two future emperors, Claudius II and Aurelian, to defeat them at the battle of Naissus (now Nis in Serbia) in 269. The victory was so complete that it was almost a century before the frontier once again had to be defended against Goths and Sarmatians. Major invasions took place but also relatively peaceful immigration, in which whole tribes fleeing the warlike Huns were allowed to settle within the Empire.

Barbarians and Christians

In the 4th and early 5th centuries, large tribes of Goths and other Germanic peoples moved into the Danubian region and weakened the Roman Empire. Worse was to follow in the 5th century when Huns from the Asian steppes, led by Attila, ravaged southeastern Europe and invaded the Roman heartland of Italy itself.

In the 6th and 7th centuries, the previously little-known Slavs from eastern Europe expanded west and southwards, and in the lands which today form Bulgaria they intermingled with the Thracian population. In the 8th century Charlemagne, Emperor of the Franks, brought much of western and central Europe under his rule, driving out the Goths and the descendants of Attila's Huns. However, Magyars from somewhere between the Volga river and the Ural mountains settled in Hungary along with a lesser number of Turkic Petchenegs.

In the 10th century ten tribes—seven Hungarian Magyars and three Khazar—united to defend themselves from menacing Petchenegs, Russians and Bulgars. Prince Arpád, head of the Magyars, was named supreme leader. Hungary's conversion to Christianity in 975, initiated under a great-grandson of Arpád, Prince Géza, made the Danube a relatively safe overland route for pilgrims going to the Holy Land. Géza's son Stephen was crowned in the year 1000 as the first king of Hungary. Canonized after his death, Stephen became the country's patron saint. The river proved rather more perilous for the huge, disorganized groups of French and Germans who set out in 1096 on the so-called People's Crusade to "save" Jerusalem from Islam. Pillaging their way through Austria and Hungary, they soon antagonized the local people and there were many skirmishes and some full-scale battles. Later crusades however brought something of an economic a boom to the towns along the banks of the Danube. England's King Richard I the Lion-Heart was imprisoned in Dürnstein Castle on his way home from Palestine in 1192. In 1396, in the so-called "Last Crusade", an army of 100,000 Germans, French, Hungarians, Poles, Bohemians, Italians and Spaniards congregated at Budapest and advanced down the Danube — to meet with a crushing defeat by the Turks at Nicopolis, now Nikopol in Bulgaria.

The Viceroy of Hungary, János (John) Hunyadi, repelled Turkish invaders (1456) at Nándorfehérvár (now Belgrade) but died, probably of the plague, in the same year. His eldest son was murdered soon afterwards and his second son Mátyás (Matthias) was chosen by the Hungarian nobles to succeed as king at the age of 15. Renowned as the "just king" Matthias I Corvinus, he

The spectacular ruins of Devín Castle in Slovakia near the border with Austria.

reigned from 1458 to 1490, regarded in Hungary as an intellectual golden age.

The Turkish Tide

In the 16th century, the Danube became the route of a "crusade" in reverse, as Suleiman the Magnificent's Ottoman Turks carried Islam west from the Black Sea. After the battle of Mohács in 1526, Hungary fell to the Ottomans for 150 years. Serbia, Bosnia and parts of Romania also came under their rule. However,

An Orthodox icon in a church in Constanța (Romania).

in spite of besieging it in 1529 and again in 1683, the Ottomans failed to take Vienna, which became the base for Austria's Habsburg rulers to undertake the gradual reconquest of Hungary by 1687, followed by Transylvania in 1691. The Treaty of Karlowitz (Sremski Karlovci) ended the war against the Turks in 1699 and made Austria the major power in the Danube region.

During the reign of Maria Theresa (1740–80), the peoples of most of the Danube region were united. The Archduchess moved German settlers into the areas that had been left deserted after the expulsion of the Turks, and these energetic newcomers introduced new methods of agriculture, developed trade and industry and built whole new villages and towns. The Ottoman Turks were not yet completely beaten; they still held large parts of the Balkans. However, in the Russo-Turkish War of 1768–74 Russia occupied the principalities of Moldavia and Walachia, and thanks to the Treaty of Svishtov (1791), Austria gained the Iron Gate pass on the Danube near Orşova. Russia conducted further wars against Turkey, some of them in the Danubian region. In the Treaty of Adrianople (Edirne) in 1829, almost all of the Danube delta was ceded to Russia.

Another important event took place in 1829: the founding of the Donau-Dampfschifffahrtsgesellschaft (Danube Steamship Company). Its operations began with a service linking Vienna and Budapest. Until World War I it was the biggest inland shipping company in the world. Under the terms of the Treaty of Paris (1856) following the Crimean War, Russia lost control of shipping on the lower Danube, which was declared open to international traffic.

In 1877 the Russian Tsar Alexander II launched another war against the Turks, with the declared aim of freeing Bulgaria from their rule. After a five month-long siege and huge loss of life on both sides, the Turkish stronghold of Pleven fell to Russian forces, and in 1878 Bulgaria became an independent state. After 1870 the Danube was rerouted around Vienna to prevent flooding.

The End of an Empire

When World War I came to an end in 1918, the Austro-Hungarian monarchy collapsed; Hungary and Czechoslovakia became independent states, and the new Kingdom of the Serbs, Croats and Slovenes (later to be known as Yugoslavia) united a large part of the Balkans. Following the founding of the European Commission of the Danube in 1856, an international Danube Commission was set up in 1921 to control traffic on the river from Ulm in southern Germany all the way to the Black Sea, and keep navigational equipment in good repair. The European Commission was the first international body to have serious police and juridical powers over private vessels and over individual people too. Both commissions were dissolved in 1940.

World War II and After

During World War II, the Danube became a battle line. German naval forces used the river to reach the Black Sea. The victorious Soviet army occupied Hungary and Romania in 1944 and marched into Belgrade, although Tito's partisans could take some of the credit for the defeat of the Germans.

In the aftermath of the war, communist regimes were imposed on the nations of Central Europe and the Balkans. Austria was divided into Soviet and western-controlled zones until 1955, when a peace agreement restored its independence as a neutral nation. In 1948, seven countries bordering the river revived the Danube Commission, which today has eleven member states. The fall of the Berlin Wall in 1989 has had far-reaching consequences for all the nations on the middle and lower Danube. The former Soviet-bloc states threw off the communist yoke, and most managed the transition to some form of democracy. The sad exception was Yugoslavia, where nationalist, ethnic and religious tensions led to its break-up. In 1999, Serbia, the largest of the six separate states that emerged from the wreck, launched an attack on its rebellious province of Kosovo, in defiance of international warnings. In response, NATO forces bombed the Danube bridges in Serbia, closing the river to shipping for some years. With all of them now rebuilt, normal commerce has been resumed, including river cruises all the way to the Black Sea.

Meanwhile, the enlargement of the EU to 28 nations has extended its reach along the whole course of the Danube: Hungary and Slovakia joined in 2004, Romania and Bulgaria in 2007 and Croatia in 2013.

The Marienberg Fortress watches over the River Main at Würzburg.

ON THE SCENE

A Danube cruise sets its own agenda. Over its entire length, the great river flows through, or past, ten Central and East-European countries. Fields, forests and picturesque villages slip by at a gentle pace. The ship ties up at a succession of charming little towns and great cities, usually close to the historic centres so you can stroll ashore to take in the principal sights.

Würzburg to Passau

Before embarking on the Danube River itself, many cruises begin on the River Main, linked to it by the man-made Main-Danube Canal. Some travellers start at Würzburg, a proud episcopal city straddling the River Main, others at Bamberg, Nuremberg or Regensburg.

Würzburg

The illustrious bishopric of Würzburg lies in the heart of Franconia's wine country. Vineyards spread up the slopes around the **Marienberg Fortress** (Festung) overlooking the town from across the Main river.

This Renaissance fortress houses the **Mainfränkisches Museum** of regional art and folklore, including ancient wine-presses. The most cherished works are the Gothic sculptures and wood-carvings of Tilman Riemenschneider, who made Würzburg his home from 1483 to 1531.

Old Town

Cross the **Old Main Bridge** (Alte Mainbrücke) to reach the Old Town on the other side of Main. Erected in the late 15th century, the bridge replaced the oldest Romanesque stone bridge in Germany, which dated from around 1120.

Neumünster

The noble façade of this fine baroque church is attributed to Johann Dientzenhofer. Inside, a Riemenschneider Madonna in stone stands in the southeast niche of the rotunda. The church is the burial shrine of St Kilian, the Irish missionary martyred in Würzburg in 689.

St Kilian Cathedral

The Cathedral is dedicated to the Irish monk. On the south side of the transept are several Riemenschneider sculptures in a modern stone setting.

Residenz

In the episcopal princes' Residenz, designed by Balthasar Neumann and Lukas von Hildebrandt (1744) and listed as a UNESCO World Heritage Site, the city possesses one of the finest baroque palaces in Germany. Giambattista Tiepolo painted the Europa fresco over the grand ceremonial staircase, as well as those in the oval **Kaisersaal** (Imperial Hall) depicting Würzburg's medieval history.

Neumann's triumph is the **Hofkirche**, the court church flooded with light and colour. Tiepolo contributed an *Assumption* and the *Angels' Fall from Heaven* for two altars.

Ochsenfurt

Another 20 km (12 miles) upstream you reach Ochsenfurt, whose town walls date from the 14th century. The timber-framed houses on Hauptstrasse with wrought-iron signs are particularly attractive. Here you will find the late-Gothic **Rathaus**, whose musical clock is the town's emblem. The **Andreaskirche** (13th –15th centuries) has a richly decorated interior with a sculpture by

Riemenschneider. Richard I of England was detained here in 1193, one of several places he was held, while returning to England from the Third Crusade.

Kitzingen

The former importance of Kitzingen is apparent from its **Rathaus** and **Falterturm** (Crooked Tower). The city is home to the **German Carnival Museum**.

Volkach

The attractive little wine-growing town of Volkach, on a loop of the Main, is worth a visit for its fine Renaissance **Town Hall** and the baroque **Schelfenhaus**, but especially for the pilgrim church of **Maria im Weingarten** (Mary-in-the-Vineyard) to the northwest of the town, which houses Riemenschneider's *Rosenkranzmadonna* (Madonna of the Rosary).

Schweinfurt

Schweinfurt is the biggest industrial centre of Lower Franconia. The city has been destroyed several times over the centuries. Nevertheless, some buildings remain to attest to its historic importance as a free imperial city: the late-Romanesque **Johanniskirche** (altered several times), the **Town Hall** (16th century), the former **Gymnasium** (grammar school), now the Museum Altes Gymnasium, and the **Zeughaus** (armoury).

ROTHENBURG OB DER TAUBER

This town south of Würzburg is the quintessence of Germany's most romantic era. Medieval ramparts, monumental gates and lofty gabled half-timbered houses, beautifully preserved, recall Rothenburg's past glories. The town is built on heights over a river valley. Begin your walk around town at the 15th-century **Ratstrinkstube** (Councillor's Tavern), now the Tourist Information Office, on the north side of Marktplatz. The figures on the old clock go into action on the hour from 10 a.m. to 10 p.m.

The imposing **Rathaus** is an apt expression of Rothenburg's civic pride during its medieval and Renaissance glory. Anyone tackling the stairs to the top of the belfry gets a splendid view over the town and Tauber valley. The Gothic **Church of St Jakob** (1311) contains the famous *Holy Blood altarpiece* (1505) by Tilman Riemenschneider.

A 750-year-old Dominican convent houses the **Reichsstadtmuseum** (Imperial City Museum). The Hohenstaufens' castle has long gone, but the **Burgtor** city gate (1360) still stands, leading to the castle gardens with a good view of the Tauber valley. The **Plönlein** or "Little Square", surrounded by timber-framed houses, is one of Rothenburg's most picturesque spots. From the **Spital**, the former hospital at the southern end of town, and the 17th-century **Spital Bastion**, you can get the best views of the well-conserved **City Wall**.

Dominique Michellod

Hassfurt

The delightful Franconian town of Hassfurt lies 28 km (17 miles) further on. Its late-Gothic **Ritterkapelle** (Knights' Chapel) is embellished by a heraldic frieze with 241 coats of arms, together with interesting tombs. The Gothic **Pfarrkirche St. Kilian** contains several works of art, including a wooden sculpture of John the Baptist by Riemenschneider.

Bamberg

The Main river reaches km 0 of the Main-Donau canal 25 km (15 miles) above Hassfurt. It is only 5 km (3 miles) from there to the episcopal town of Bamberg, which is listed as a UNESCO World Heritage Site since 1993. Its historic centre is graced with works by Riemenschneider and the architect family Dientzenhofer.

Take a look at the **Cathedral** (Kaiserdom St. Peter und St. Georg), where the transition from Romanesque to Gothic can be clearly traced. It houses the tomb of Emperor Heinrich II and his wife, a work by Riemenschneider, as well as the Bamberger Reiter, a Gothic equestrian statue.

On Karolinenplatz stands the late-Gothic **Alte Hofhaltung** (the former episcopal palace, now housing the historical museum), as well as the early baroque Neue Hofhaltung (also called the **Neue Residenz**). The latter, designed by

Bayreuth. Make a side-trip to Bayreuth, on the Red Main river in Upper Franconia, known for its annual festival of Richard Wagner's operas. The festival was founded by the composer himself in 1876. His home, Villa Wahnfried, has been converted into the **Richard Wagner Museum** (currently closed for refurbishment). Wagner is buried in the garden with his wife Cosima.

The UNESCO-listed **Markgräfliches Opernhaus** (Margravial Opera House), by two 18th-century theatre designers from Bologna, is a charming baroque creation in the Old Town, with three galleries festooned in stucco trimmings (closing for four years' renovation from end 2012). The Opera House includes the New Palace, built between 1753 and 1754.

istockphoto.com/Domes

J.L. Dientzenhofer, has on the first floor a gallery of paintings by German masters, and on the second you can admire grand chambers with antique furniture and tapestries. There's a fine view of the old town and the **Kloster Michaelsberg**, the Benedictine abbey of St Michael, from the charming **Rosengarten**, planted with 4,500 roses.

On an artificial island near the **Obere Brücke** (Upper Bridge) stands the remarkable **Altes Rathaus** (Old Town Hall), its façade decorated with 18th-century frescoes. Inside are precious porcelain objects from the Ludwig Collection. Its central position was due to the fact that it served the bourgeois community of one bank and the episcopal community of the other.

The picturesque fishing quarter of **Klein-Venedig**, "Little Venice", lies on the right bank of the Regnitz river. At the end of August, the old town is the site of an exuberant fair.

Main-Danube Canal

In 1992 the boldest dreams of Charlemagne and Ludwig I of Bavaria were realised when the 171 km (106 mile) Main–Danube Canal between Bamberg and Kelheim was completed, opening to seagoing ships a 3, 500 km (2,170 mile) waterway linking the North Sea with the Black Sea.

istockphoto.com/Busto

Bamberg's well-preserved Old Town Hall (1386).

At the end of the 8th century, Charlemagne ordered the construction of the "Caroline Trench" which showed a real prowess in technique for the times, but the work was abandoned. After the Thirty Years' War (1618–1648), ambitious new projects came to light — amongst them was the canal to link the Main with the Danube. The plans were only put into operation years later, to promote industrial development. Inaugurated with great pomp in 1846, the Ludwig Canal, 172 km (106 miles) in length, is the

STEP BY STEP

Inserted with respect in the landscape at the south-east tip of Germany, the **Main-Danube Canal**'s fascinating flight of locks creates the link between the two rivers (across the range of Franconian Alb hills to Bamberg and beyond). It takes five levels to negotiate the rise of just 68 m from **Kelheim** over a distance of 55 km to just beyond Bachhausen, where the canal maintains for a stretch of 16.5 km to the far side of **Hilpoltstein** what is the highest summit level of a navigable canal of this size in Europe. This is where ships also cross the watershed between the Rhine and Danube. The Hilpoltstein lock begins the descent. After a further eleven levels over a stretch of 100 km, the ships reach **Bamberg**. The shortest barrage measures 3.7 km, the longest 20.43 km. The drops in height vary between just 5.3 m to an impressive 24.5 m and overcome in all an altitude difference of 165 m. For this, the locks are handled by only four remote-control centres.

At the port of Bamberg, 230 m above sea level, it continues on the Main, which winds its way westwards in countless bends through splendid landscapes, villages and towns. Destination: **Mainz-Kostheim**, 388 km away, where it meets up with its big brother, the Rhine; 34 barrages line up to overcome a total drop of about 157 m. The altitude drops vary between 2.36 m and 7.6 m. Almost all the locks are linked to hydro-electric power plants, but fishing passes, too. The shortest tail section measures 5.11 km, the longest 18.8 km.

If you compare both ends (or beginnings) of the waterway, you can ascertain that the Rhine at Mainz is 263 m lower than the Danube at Kelheim. It is marvellous to note how the carefully thought through facilities and their technical achievements fit so harmoniously into their natural surroundings and offer an almost silent and peaceful navigation route. A country experience away from the hustle and bustle.

predecessor of the current Main–Danube Canal. Not being large enough, it met with increasing competition from the railways. Further work was undertaken in 1922 and the new Mindorf section was built but the war put a temporary stop to construction, which only recommenced in 1960. If the northern section, stretching from Bamberg to Nuremberg, became navigable in 1972, it was only in 1992 that the final stretch to Kelheim was inaugurated. Leaving aside all the technical achievements, a trip on the Main and the Danube is first and foremost a chance to experience a unique landscape and an opportunity to make acquaintance with the customs and culture of Franconia and Bavaria.

Nuremberg
A fine-looking town, Nuremberg can once more look with pride on its distinguished history. A centre of medieval culture and veritable heart of Renaissance art north of the Alps, it has also always been at the forefront of German industry and commerce. Today, the city dominates the northern Bavarian region of Franconia.

Altstadt (Old Town)
Opposite the Tiergärtner Gate *(Tor)*, the **Albrecht Dürer's House** was bought by the painter in 1509, who lived there until his death in 1528. Guided tours can be taken.

The 17th century **Rathaus** has a façade worthy of an Italian palace. The **Sebalduskirche** was built in the 8th and 9th centuries

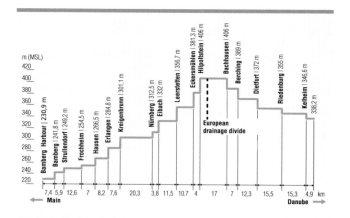

and stands on the other side of the Rathausplatz. Over at Burgstrasse 15, the **Stadtmuseum Fembohaus** (1596) is a magnificent example of Renaissance architecture.

The old town's numerous fountains include the 16th century **Gänsemännchenbrunnen** in the Rathausplatz and the **Schöner Brunnen** in the Hauptmarkt (marketplace). In the same place, and restored to its former majesty, is the **Frauenkirche**—the stepped gable 14th century church destroyed in 1945.

Museums

The **Germanisches Nationalmuseum**, dating from 1852, is housed in a Carthusian monastery on the Kornmarkt. With over a million objects, it is the largest German museum of art and history. Several minutes away by foot, opposite the central station, the **Neues Museum – Staatliches Museum für Kunst und Design** (National Art and Design Museum) applies two visions: pure and applied art.

The **Verkehrmuseum Nürnberg** (Transport Museum) at Lessingstrasse 6 consists of two museums: the **DB Museum** (Railway Museum) and the **Museum für Kommunikation** (Museum of Communication). The **Spielzeugmusem** (Toy Museum) at Karlstrasse 13 presents a wonderful array of historical toys and leads right through to the high-tech games of today.

Riedenburg

The present-day health resort of Riedenburg (km 152) on the River Altmühl became a market town in the 13th century. The **Altmühl Valley Nature Park** is popular with hikers, canoeists and cyclists alike. The Falconry Lodge at **Schloss Rosenburg** (Rosenburg Castle, built 1112) gives demonstrations with large birds of prey.

Kelheim

Close to Kelheim (km 168 on the Main-Danube Canal, km 2414 on the Danube) the Altmühl flows into the Danube; this is the end of the Main–Danube Canal. Note the Gothic **Mariä Himmelfahrt Parish Church** and the elegant façades of the baroque town houses. To the west of Kelheim, the **Befreiungshalle**, built by Ludwig I to commemorate the wars of liberation fought against Napoleon, crowns the Michelsberg.

Following the Danube to Austria

From Kelheim it is possible to navigate the Danube through breathtaking landscapes as far as Passau.

Weltenburg Monastery

This Benedictine monastery stands in a setting full of natural drama, just where the Danube breaks the so-called **Danube Gorge** through the hills of the Franconian Alb (km 2419).

Regensburg (Ratisbon)

Regensburg (km 2380) reveals itself in full historical splendour. Its nearly intact medieval centre is UNESCO listed.

The city hails back to Roman times, when the mighty **Porta Praetoria** was built (vestiges can be seen in the north wing of the Bischofshof). The diocese was founded in the 8th century, and from this time princes and emperors held their Diets in the city. Regensburg's heyday was the Middle Ages, and to this day the magnificence of the merchants' houses attests to their wealth and prestige.

The **Steinerne Brücke** (Stone Bridge) is the oldest surviving bridge in Germany (12th century) and connects the main part of the city with the settlement on the other bank of the Danube.

The old city is dominated by the magnificent **Dom St. Peter**, with its 105-m towers, the *pièce de résistance* of Gothic architecture in Bavaria. The cathedral houses many treasures. The finest secular building in the city is probably the **Altes Rathaus** (Old Town Hall).

St Emmeram's Basilica dates back to the 8th century but has the Asam brothers to thank for its sumptuous Baroque interior.

The **Museum of Danube Shipping** (Donau-Schifffahrts-Museum) focuses on river shipping on the Danube and other rivers.

fotolia.com/Vieraugen

The Benedictine Monastery of Weltenburg, located right on the Danube Gorge.

Walhalla

A short distance downstream, a huge white marble pseudo-Grecian temple towers above the Danube: this is Walhalla, built for Ludwig I of Bavaria.

Straubing

On Hauptplatz in the picturesque Altstadt (Old Town), see the 14th-century **Stadtturm** (City Tower) with its five spires. Theresienplatz and Ludwigsplatz are surrounded by patrician houses. One of the finest churches is the **Ursulinenkirche**, by the Asam brothers. A short distance out of town is Straubing's oldest place of worship, the **Peterskirche**, built around 1180. One of the churchyard's three chapels is devoted to Agnes Bernauer, a barber's daughter who fell in love with Albrecht III of Bavaria, and was drowned in the Danube when the duke's father heard of their marriage.

The Danube traces a hairpin loop at Schlögen.

Passau to Vienna

The "Town of Three Rivers", Passau, stands at the confluence of the Danube, the Inn joining it from the south and the little Ilz from the north. Champions of the Inn (which gives its name to Innsbruck) note that it is broader and bluer here than the Danube, and so much more deserving of Johann Strauss's waltz. Ships moor below the proud Veste Oberhaus castle, and Austria is but a stone's throw away.

Passau

On the German side of the border, Passau (km 2227) is a solid old bishopric that has always enjoyed the good life, celebrating its religious festivities with plenty of music, beer, and hot chocolate for the children. Historically prospering from trade in wine, wheat and salt, it is an inviting city, from the bulbous onion domes and graceful arches of its baroque monuments to the rounded promontories separating the waterways.

The core of the town stands on the ridge of land between the Danube and Inn rivers. Towering over it is the **Stephansdom**, with its three onion domes, flamboyant Gothic chancel and rich baroque interior which can claim a total of 1,000 sculpted figures. The church is the seat of the Catholic Bishop of Passau. The church organ, built in the early 20th century, is the world's largest cathedral organ.

The Gothic **Town Hall** and the Bohemian glassware of the **Glasmuseum** (Glass Museum) are equally worth a visit. Nearby in a westerly direction, the **Museum of Modern Art Wörlen** (MMK) hosts prominent changing exhibitions.

From the hilltop position of the **Paulinerkloster Mariahilf** (Pauline Father's Monastery of Mariahilf), reached via the Heavenly Ladder (*Wallfahrtsstiege*) leaving from the city centre, you can contemplate a spectacular panorama.

From the **Veste Oberhaus** castle, which today houses a medieval museum, the view looks down upon the jetty and the vessels below.

Passau's pacifists. The people of Passau have always been far too fond of the good life to spoil it by wasting time fighting. When the town was besieged by the Bavarians in 1703, the bishop's three companies of soldiers declined to report for duty, explaining that they had all come down with a fever. The Bavarian forces were eventually able to complete their conquest, but not until 1741—and their general, much frustrated, complained that he had met no opposition at all!

Through the Mühl Region

At **Lindau** (km 2222), where more Danube cruise ships dock on the German left bank, as far as the **Jochenstein power station** (lock at km 2203), the river forms the German-Austrian border. For the next 323 km, it flows through Austria, at first through the wooded hill country of the Upper Austrian Mühlviertel. River travellers are charmed here by medieval villages, knights' castles, monasteries and the splendid narrow loop of the **Schlögener Schlinge** or "Loop" (km 2187). The hydroelectric power stations of Aschach (km 2162) and Ottensheim-Wilhering (km 2147) oblige ships to pass once more through locks. Upper Austria borders the Czech Republic, where one can see such splendid sites as the UNESCO-listed Old City of **Český Krumlov**.

Linz

The city stands at an important crossroads for traffic to Germany and the Czech Republic. With a population of 194,000, Linz is the provincial capital of Upper Austria. In 1832, the province's first horse-drawn tramway was inaugurated here, leading to České Budějovice (Budweis) in Bohemia. Five years later, the first steamship docked in Linz. In addition, this is also the centre of Austria's steel industry.

On the right bank of the Danube, the **Lentos Kunstmuseum** (Art Museum) catches your eye. The modern style of the building, designed by Swiss architects Weber & Hofer, is matched by the contemporary art of its exhibitions. At night the "Swiss Box" lights up blue or red: in daytime, you can look from the city side through the

"Danube Window", a large aperture in the middle of the building, at the picturesque landscape on the other river bank, where a second glass building; the **Ars Electronica Center** comes into view. The Centre was opened in 2009, the year that Linz was named Europe's culture capital. Today it is the town's most popular museum. The futuristic edifice is appropriate for its theme—the world of humanity and its changes. In several labs, the visitor gains new insights into time, the planet, robots and even cloned plants.

In 2013, Linz inaugurated its house of music, the **Musiktheater Am Volksgarten**—Europe's most modern opera house—forging a link with its rich musical past: Mozart composed his "Linz" Symphony here, Beethoven his 8th Symphony; the great Anton Bruckner (1824–1896) was born not far from Linz and was organist in the Old Cathedral until he moved to Vienna in 1868.

Other testimonies to the past are the Gothic **Town Hall** and the pastel-coloured 17th- and 18th-century houses on the **Hauptplatz** (main square) which forms the heart of the Old Town. In the middle of the square is the tall **Dreifaltigkeitssäule** (Trinity Pillar) erected to commemorate the deliverance of the town from war, fire and the plague. The carillon rings out several times each day. The Baroque Jesuit Church is also known as the **Alter Dom** (Old Cathedral). Not far from the Hauptplatz, the elegant Renaissance **Landhaus**, built between 1568 and 1658, is the seat of Upper Austria's provincial government. The **Schlossmuseum** (Castle Museum)

SALZBURG

A golden city, home of Mozart and echoing to a thousand other musical themes, Salzburg lies on the left bank of the River Salzach and the Mönchsberg, topped by the Hohensalzburg fortress. The oldest part of the town has been claimed a heritage site by UNESCO.

There is something indefinably southern about the old part of town which many compare with Florence or Venice. Baroque architecture lends a dreamy, poetic charm. Narrow streets lead into spacious squares, elegant settings for Gothic churches and monasteries and ornately sculpted fountains. Mansions and Renaissance palaces reign over beautiful parks and gardens.

Today Mozart haunts Salzburg. Recitals are held in the most splendid ceremonial rooms of the palaces and castles; his homes are preserved as museums. There's the Mozarteum music academy, the annual festival, and even chocolates, Mozartkugeln. The 250th anniversary of his birth in 2006 was marked by a host of events and celebrations.

A good place to start exploring is the heart of the Old Town. In the centre of **Residenzplatz** stands a large baroque fountain (1658–61) surrounded by rearing horses. At 7 a.m., 11 a.m. and 6 p.m., familiar melodies by Mozart ring out on the 35 bells of the 17th-century **Glockenspiel**, on the east side of the square. The west side is taken up by the Residenz, a palace of the arch-bishops founded in 1120 (the present buildings date from the 17th and 18th centuries). The south side of Residenzplatz is dominated by the huge **Dom** (Cathedral). It was built in Italian Renaissance style, with baroque overtones, between 1614 and 1655. In the first side chapel to the left of the entrance, is the Romanesque font, supported by four bronze lions, where baby Mozart was christened in 1756.

The **Rupertinum**, a baroque 17th-century palace built by Paris Lodron, occupies four floors and has been perfectly adapted inside to house graphic art and photographic collections. It forms an integral part of the Museum of Modern Art.

Backing into the base of the Mönchsberg, the long building of the **Grosses Festspielhaus** (Great Festival Hall) has been converted from the former court stables. It includes several theatres, the Haus für Mozart and other concert halls, and a riding school with three rows of seats carved out of the hillside. The 130 horses that were quartered in these palatial lodgings had the exclusive rights to the waters of the **Pferdeschwemme** on nearby Sigmundsplatz. A grandiose Renaissance structure of 1695, this splendid horse trough is ornamented with frescoes of prancing steeds, dominated by a vigorous sculpted group by Michael Bernhard Mandl depicting a man breaking in a horse.

Getreidegasse is the great shopping street of Salzburg's old town. A veritable forest of wrought-iron guild signs adorns its Renaissance and baroque façades. The houses are narrow but four or five storeys high and delving deep on each side, around alleyways and hidden courtyards.

Number 9 is **Mozart's Birthplace** (Geburtshaus) — now an enchanting museum. Exhibits include manuscripts of minuets Mozart wrote when he was five, his counterpoint notebook, paintings of father Leopold and sister Nannerl. A clavichord bears a note written by wife Constanze: "On this piano my dear departed husband Mozart composed *The Magic Flute*".

Getreidegasse opens onto Rathausplatz; continue past the Town Hall to the **Alter Markt** on your right. At No. 6, don't miss the Old Pharmacy (**Alte Hofapotheke**) that has kept its old rococo décor. At No. 8, Makartplatz, Mozart's Residence, the **Mozarts Wohnhaus**, was the family home from 1773 to 1780. It has been converted into a Mozart museum. **Dreifaltigkeitskirche** (Trinity Church), with a concave façade, is another of Fischer van Erlach's baroque masterpieces (1694–1702). The building on the west side of the square is the **State Theatre**; behind it is the **Marionettentheater** where puppets perform *The Magic Flute*. The **Mozarteum** Academy of Music is just next door.

Corbis/Bianchetti

SALZKAMMERGUT

A popular round-trip east of Salzburg takes you to the lakes and spas of the Salzkammergut. On the shore of a crescent-shaped lake beneath the steep slopes of the Drachenwand and Schafberg mountains, the town of **Mondsee** grew up around a 15th-century Benedictine abbey. Some of its buildings serve as a museum recounting the life of the neolithic inhabitants of the lake region. At the southern tip of the Mondsee, a succession of tunnels and narrow roads overhung by rocks form a pass between Scharfling and **St. Gilgen**, a resort prized for its water sports facilities on Wolfgangsee. Mozart's mother was born here. You can take a paddle-steamer from St Gilen to the town of **St. Wolfgang**. A place of pilgrimage since the 12th century, St Wolfgang's church has a fine altarpiece by Michael Pacher, completed in 1481, depicting the coronation of the Virgin. The famous White Horse Inn *(Weisses Rössl)* set to music by Ralph Benatzky is here, on the lakefront. East of St Wolfgang, **Bad Ischl** was one of Europe's greatest cultural centres during the reign of Franz-Joseph, who spent his summers here. In his wake came all the big names of the 19th-century art and music world: Johann Strauss, Brahms, Franz Lehar, Nestroy, Anton Bruckner and so on. Today you can visit the emperor's villa (Kaiservilla). Empress Sissi preferred the little marble castle (Marmorschlössl) in the park, now a photography museum. South of Bad Ischl, **Hallstatt** is one of the most picturesque of Austrian villages, a cluster of white houses squeezed between the lake and the wooded slopes of the **Dachstein**. Its salt was extracted as far back as neolithic times, as you will learn in the local museum. The historic Hallstatt-Dachstein / Salzkammergut cultural landscape is listed as a UNESCO World Heritage Site. North of Bad Ischl, the road through the **Traun Valley** was one of the great European salt routes. The section between Ebensee and Traunkirchen is hewn into the rock high above the **Traunsee**, Austria's deepest lake. At its northern end, **Gmunden** has an island castle linked to the shore by a wooden walkway. The scenic route back to Salzburg takes you across to **Steinbach am Attersee** then follows the east shore of the lake. Make a halt at the lookout point at **Buchberg**.

above the Danube houses the archaeological and historical art collections of Upper Austria's provincial museum.

The **Martinskirche**, founded in 799 and rebuilt in the 10th century, counts among Austria's most ancient houses of worship.

A steep ride from the Hauptplatz takes you in 20 minutes to the **Pöstlingberg** on the north bank, Linz's "hometown-mountain", from which you have a good view of the city and the environs.

Linz to Mauthausen

Beyond the extensive Linz harbour and river mouth of the Traun come the locks at the Abwinden-Asten power plant (km 2120).

Mauthausen (km 2112), originally established as an imperial customs station at the confluence with the Enns river, is now more bitterly remembered as the site of Austria's largest concentration camp. A chapel and a monument remember its 100,000 victims. Just 17 km (10.5 miles) further, there are more locks at the Wallsee-Mitterkirchen power plant.

Strudengau

The Strudengau is a quite craggy and once dangerous stretch of river between Dornach and Persenbeug (km 2060). **Greinburg Castle** watches over the enchanting town of **Grein** (km 2079), which has a rococo theatre in the

Touristeninformation Linz

The Lentos Kunstmuseum at Linz is housed in a modern building on the right bank.

main square. The theatre has remained unaltered since it was built in 1790. **Werfenstein Castle** in Struden (km 2076) and the picturesque ruin of **Freyenstein** on the right bank (km 2070) are also worth a look.

Schloss Persenbeug—a baroque castle of the Habsburgs—stands on the left bank near the locks of the Ybbs-Persenbeug hydroelectric station.

Nibelungengau

The hydroelectric station is the start of one of the Danube's most romantic sections. For 24 km (15 miles), from Ybbs to Emmersdorf an der Donau, the river flows through the Nibelungengau (Land of the Nibelungs), source of inspiration for Wagner's operas. The baroque church of **Maria Taferl** above Marbach (km 2050) is the most important pilgrimage church in Lower Austria.

Wachau

The locks of the Melk power station (km 2038) herald the beginning of Wachau, a stretch of the Danube Valley which is listed as a UNESCO World Heritage Site. Here the Danube conjures up dreamy thoughts in the hardiest of folk as it winds its way just 30 km (19 miles) between Melk and Krems in Lower Austria (Niederösterreich), where country villages alternate with dark castle ruins on craggy cliffs. This stretch basks in an exceptionally mild climate, suitable for premium wine grape cultivation. The Wachau is easily accessible from Vienna by road or by Danube steamship.

Melk

Melk, an amazing landmark of the Wachau valley, is best known for its massive Benedictine Abbey.

The City

Long before Melk (km 2036) became the home of the Benedictines in 1089, its clifftop position above the river bend made it an ideal military camp from which to fend off barbarians. Melk was settled permanently as early as the 9th century, and the Babenbergs made it their royal residence and stronghold in the 10th, although it was not to receive a charter until 1898.

In the Middle Ages, the salt, wine and iron trades flourished here, their products carried by Danube shipping. In 1548 a fire reduced the town virtually to ashes, and it was rebuilt in the Renaissance style.

Melk Abbey

Having crossed the forecourt, you find yourself confronted by the impressive eastern façade of the monastery. This dates from the early 18th century, when Jakob Prandtauer was commissioned to transform the forbidding strategic fortification into a splendid baroque sanctuary with gracefully tapering towers and a majestic octagonal dome. The project was completed after his death by his pupil Josef Munggenast.

The **Marble Hall** (Marmorsaal), light, bright and richly decorated with ceiling frescoes and other ornaments, was used as a dining room and guest room in former days. Pass through the balconies overlooking the Danube to the **Library** (Bibliothek), its magnificent inlaid shelves weighed down with some 100,000 precious books and 2,000 manuscripts. The room is a work of art in its own right.

A spiral staircase leads down into the **Abbey Church** (Stiftskirche), where you can admire the high altar, the pulpit, the beautifully carved confessionals and choir stalls, the ceiling frescoes by Johann Michael Rottmayr and the great organ.

The Treasury includes the *Cross of Melk* inlaid with pearls and precious stones. It is claimed that the cross was stolen in the 12th century. It found its way back to the monastery by mysterious means —floating against the current upstream from Vienna! It can be seen on special occasions.

Between Melk and Dürnstein

Schönbühel Castle stands on a rock on the right bank (km 2032). The medieval **Aggstein** robber barons' castle is perched in ruin on a rugged hilltop (km 2025).

Across the river in **Willendorf** (km 2024) the famous *Venus of Willendorf* fertility statue was found (on display in the Naturhistorisches Museum in Vienna).

The attractive wine village of **Spitz** (km 2019) awaits with its Hinterhaus medieval castle. The parish church at **Weissenkirchen**, surrounded by vineyards, combines fortifications with a house of worship (km 2013).

Dürnstein

This pretty little baroque town (km 2009) nestles on the bank of the Danube and can only be explored on foot: cars must be left on the edge of town.

Melk Abbey and the ornate ceiling of its Marble Hall. | **The banks of the Danube are popular with cyclists.**

Kuenringer Castle

Dürnstein is famous for the castle above the town in which Richard I of England, the Lionheart, was held captive in 1192. He had offended the Babenberg Duke Leopold V during the Third Crusade, and was captured in Vienna whilst attempting to slip away up the Danube valley. According to the legend, his faithful minstrel Blondel traced him here to Dürnstein by singing the his favourite songs outside every castle until he came to the right one and heard Richard join in the chorus, but the captive was only released after the payment of a huge ransom.

In 1645, during the Thirty Years' War, Swedish troops burned Dürnstein, leaving the castle in ruins. The 20-min ascent to the castle is rewarded with fine views of the river.

Abbey Church

The Stiftskirche, resplendent in blue and white, has one of the finest baroque towers in the whole of Austria. Walk through the ornate portal and the quiet courtyard to reach the interior, where the three divine virtues Faith, Hope and Charity watch over the carved pulpit. The cloister is worth a visit.

Hauptstrasse

On Hauptstrasse, bounded to the east by the **Kremser Tor** (gate), you can see many pretty town houses from the 16th to 18th centuries, some of them with sgraffito decoration. On the same street, you will find the late-Gothic **Town Hall** with its fine courtyard. The ruins of the former **Klarissenkloster** (Convent of the Poor Clares) have been incorporated into a hotel.

Kellerschlössl

You can take part in a wine tasting in the Kellerschlössl (1715), with its huge old wine cellar and rich decoration of frescoes.

Krems an der Donau

The centre of the Wachau's wine industry, Krems (km 2002), linked to Stein by the village of Und ("and" in German) is considered to be the most beautiful town in Lower Austria. The three towns have merged into one. If you walk along Untere Landstrasse, past the Kleines Sgraffitohaus, you will come to the Simandlbrunnen ("Simon's Fountain"), depicting the character in question returning home from an evening's drinking to a none-too-gentle reception from his angry wife.

Cross Wegscheid to reach Hoher Markt, the town's oldest square. Here stands the resplendent Gothic Gozzoburg, a patrician residence built in the 13th century in Italian style by the municipal judge Gozzo. Medieval pageants are held here. In the Piaristenkirche, the church in Piaristengasse, there's an extensive collection of paintings by Martin Johann Schmidt (1718–1801), a prolific artist familiarly known as Kremser Schmidt, who adorned most of the region's churches.

The Pfarrkirche St Veit (St Vitus parish church), known as "Dom der Wachau", is a fine 18th century baroque building decorated by eminent artists. The large ceiling frescoes and the All Souls Altar, at the back of the church and to the right, are by Kremser Schmidt. The Dominican church and its adjacent monastic buildings today house the Museumkrems,

which traces the development of wine-production and the town's history, including a scale model. Exhibitions and concerts are held in the early Gothic interior of the medieval church.

The **Steiner Tor**, the gate at the end of Obere Landstrasse, was part of the medieval city wall. Its round Gothic towers date from the 15th century. For many, the most enjoyable monuments in Krems are the Renaissance houses on **Obere Landstrasse**, where they serve the new Heuriger wine in tree-shaded courtyards.

Stein

In Stein, several fine buildings face Steiner Landstrasse. The **Minoritenkirche** or Minorites' Church was built during the transition from Romanesque to Gothic, and this stylistic blend gives the building its particular character. The **Passauerhof** near the Ursulakpelle (4, Pfarrplatz) is also worth a visit. The mighty seven-storey tower of the **Frauenbergkirche** rises above the town.

Göttweig Abbey

Visible from far away, Göttweig Abbey looks almost unreal sitting on its hill 425 m high a few kilometres south of the Danube. This important Benedictine monastery was founded in the 11th century and rebuilt in baroque style in the 18th century.

Altenwörth to Tulln

Ships pass through locks at the hydroelectric power plant of **Altenwörth** (km 1980). Following a popular referendum in 1979, the nuclear power station at **Zwentendorf** (km 1977) was not linked up to the national power grid.

The town of **Tulln an der Donau** (km 1963) was once the Roman cavalry post of Comagena, later an important medieval trade centre.

Klosterneuburg

Klosterneuburg Monastery was founded in 1114 and rebuilt by Emperor Karl VI in the 18th century to emulate the Escorial in Madrid, home of his Spanish Habsburg ancestors. His dream of a vast baroque palace-cum-church with nine domes, each graced with a Habsburg crown, had to stop short at one big dome, with the imperial crown, and one little one, with the crown of the Austrian archduke. The major attraction of the interior is the Leopold Chapel's superb 12th-century Verdun Altar with its 45 Biblical scenes painted in enamel panels.

The new **Essl Museum** (1, An der Donau-Au), dedicated to contemporary art, focuses mainly on Austrian art from 1945 onwards. It also offers a broad insight into the young art scene in and beyond Germany.

Vienna

The population of Vienna, Austria's capital, reflects the cosmopolitan mix of peoples once ruled by the Habsburg Empire: Hungarians, Germans, Czechs, Slovaks, Poles, Spaniards, Flemings and Italians. They have all made a contribution to the city's architecture, music and painting.

At km 1934, the narrow **Danube Canal** forks off towards the Vienna city centre (Innenstadt), but heavy river traffic stays on the main river. The city's striking modern landmarks south of the Vienna Woods—the round **Millennium Tower** (km 1932) on the right bank and the **UNO-City** complex (km 1929) beyond the artificial Danube Island on the left bank—rise up until you reach the landing stages near the **Reichsbrücke** (km 1928).

Stephansdom

With its Romanesque western façade, Gothic tower and baroque altars, the cathedral is a marvellous example of the Viennese genius for harmonious compromise, melding the austerity, dignity and exuberance of those great architectural styles.

From the north tower you have a fine view of the city, and of the huge **Pummerin** bell cast from melted-down Turkish cannons after the 1683 siege was repelled.

Mozarthaus

Wolfgang Amadeus Mozart (1756–91) and his wife Constanze lived in this pretty house from 1784 to 1787, and it was here that Mozart composed *The Marriage of Figaro* in 1785. It is his only surviving Viennese residence.

Renata Holzbachová

Wien Tourismus/MAXUM

Österreich Werbung

Kärntner Strasse and the Ring

From Stephansdom, Kärntner Strasse heads southwest; many of Vienna's smartest shops can be found on this thoroughfare. It leads past the world-famous **Staatsoper** to the **Ring**. This boulevard encircling the Innere Stadt was mapped out in the 1860s along the ramparts. Along it are handsome buildings such as the neo-Gothic **Votivkirche**, the **University** and **Rathaus** (Town Hall). On the Innere Stadt side is the **Burgtheater**, a high temple of the German stage. Beyond it is the lovely **Volksgarten** (literally, People's Garden). From the Staatsoper, walk northwards to Albertinaplatz and on to the Hofburg.

Albertina, the world's greatest graphic art collection, includes hundreds of works by masters such as Leonardo da Vinci, Dürer, Raphael, Michelangelo and Rembrandt, and 20th-century artists like Klimt and Schiele.

The Hofburg

The most imposing of the imperial palaces is the Hofburg, home of Austria's rulers since the 13th century. Take the guided tour of the **Kaiserappartements** (Imperial

Schloss Schönbrunn put into in perspective. | Social life in winter is ruled by glamorous balls. | Distinguished members of the Spanish Riding School.

Sissi: myth and reality. Empress Elisabeth (1837–98) was an intelligent and cultivated woman who worried little about court etiquette and much about the destiny of the Hungarian people. After her marriage to her cousin Franz Joseph at the age of 16, she had to exchange a hitherto fairly free life in Bavaria for the strict supervision of her mother-in-law, Sophie. The empress fell ill, probably with a venereal disease acquired from her husband, and took refuge in the milder climate of Madeira — the first of a long series of journeys abroad. In June 1867, the imperial couple were crowned King and Queen of Hungary: the dual monarchy was born. Even this, however, did not keep Sissi in the palace. After she had given her husband four children, she decided at 40 to distance herself still further from court and pursue her passion for poetry and travel. The empress suffered a terrible blow in 1889 when her son, Rudolf, apparently committed suicide on the royal estate of Mayerling, along with his mistress, Baroness Maria Vetsera. Nine years later, when out walking on the Quai du Mont-Blanc in Geneva, Elisabeth was stabbed to death by the Italian anarchist Luigi Lucheni.

Apartments), entrance on Michaelerplatz. Some rooms of the Imperial Apartments now comprise the **Sissi Museum**.

The **Burgkapelle** (Castle Chapel), tucked away in the northern corner of the Schweizerhof, was built in 1449. The Vienna Boys' Choir (Wiener Sängerknaben) sings Mass here every Sunday morning, except in July and August.

In the **Spanische Hofreitschule** (Spanish Riding School), white Lippizaner horses are trained to walk and dance with a delicacy that many ballet-dancers might envy.

Schönbrunn Palace

Protected as a UNESCO World Heritage Site, Schloss Schöbrunn is representative of the serene personality of one woman — Maria Theresa, Archduchess of Austria, Queen of Bohemia and Hungary.

Visit the **Schlosspark** (Caste Gardens) first. The park, laid out in the classical French manner, is dominated by the **Gloriette**, a neo-classical colonnade perched on the crest of a hill. It was built in 1775 to commemorate the 1757 victory over the Prussian army. The view looking over the palace with Vienna in the background makes the climb well worthwhile.

The Vienna Philharmonic Orchestra's New Year concert is always a resounding success.

In the palace itself you will see, among other splendours, the little Hall of Mirrors (Spiegelsaal) in which Mozart gave one of his first recitals at the age of 6, in 1762. The apartments of Franz Joseph and Elisabeth as well as the fifteen reception halls are in the palace's right wing. The rooms are richly furnished, draped with brocade, the walls decorated with baroque panelling in beige and gold and hung with gleaming lacquerware and mirrors.

Museums

Vienna's museum scene is rich and plentiful, but if you don't have the luxury of time you should choose the two Belvedere Palaces south of the Inner City.

The **Unteres Belvedere** (Lower Belvedere) served as Prince Eugène's summer residence; he settled there after the capture of Belgrade in 1716. Its many ceremonial halls include the Marmorgalerie (Marble Gallery), the Goldkabinett (Gold Cabinet), where a statue of Prince Eugène is reflected an infinite number of times in huge gold-framed mirrors, and the Groteskensaal (Hall of Grotesques). The Lower Belvedere and the **Orangery** host temporary exhibitions, whilst the Prunkstall (Palace Stables) are dedicated to sacred medieval art.

Entrance to the **Oberes Belvedere** (Upper Belvedere) is through an elegant gateway flanked by two lions. The Upper Belvedere houses art treasures dating from the baroque and medieval periods. The impressive Gustav Klimt collection includes his famous painting, *The Kiss*, and there are works by Egon Schiele, Oskar Kokoschka and Makart.

The **MAK**, Museum of Applied Arts (Museum für angewandte Kunst), was built from 1867 to 1871. It is a show-place for the celebrated Wiener Werkstätte (Vienna Workshops), but also for

Gustav Klimt. Klimt (1862–1918) was a pioneer of modern painting in Vienna. In 1897 he became first president of the Secession group, which gathered several young artists in search of new means of expression. Having assimilated the innovative ideas and spirit of the Impressionists, Symbolists and Pre-Raphaelites, as well as the precepts of Art Nouveau, he developed a powerful personal style, at once opulent and disquieting. Among his major works, one version of *The Kiss* is displayed at the Belvedere, while his 34-m-long Beethoven frieze can be seen in the basement of the Secession pavilion.

Österreichische Galerie Belvedere Wien

collections of handicraft and design from the world over.

Vienna-born painter and architect Hundertwasser designed the **Kunst Haus Wien – Museum Hundertwasser**, in the 3rd district, using recycled material and ceramics.

The museum displays a collection of the artist's works. The **Hundertwasserhaus**, a colourful apartment block in Löwengasse, is a shining example of non-conformism and respect for the environment.

Behind Fischer von Erlach's pink façade of the former Imperial stables, the modern **MuseumsQuartier** (district) is one of the biggest cultural complexes in the world, with museums, theatres and exhibition halls. Among these, the black basalt **Museum of Modern Art** (MUMOK), by architects Ortner & Ortner, displays modern and contemporary art, including paintings by Klee, Léger, Kandinsky, Magritte and Kokoschka, sculptures by Brancusi, Giacometti and Max Ernst. The **Leopold Museum** houses a large collection of paintings and drawings by Egon Schiele, who died in 1918 aged 28, whereas the **ZOOM Kindermuseum**, dedicated to children up to 14, offers a year-round program of exhibitions and interactive workshops.

You can also visit the city's "personal" museums, which include the **Haydnhaus** (19, Haydngasse), **Beethoven-Pasqualatihaus** (8, Mölkerbastei) and the **Sigmund Freud Museum** at Berggasse 19. Music lovers will appreciate Schubert's house museum, the **Schubert Geburtshouse** (54, Nussdorfer Straße), where the composer spent the first years of his childhood.

Wienerwald

The Vienna Woods, a popular recreation area designated a Biosphere Reserve by UNESCO, are perfect for long walks beneath the pine trees. The scenery in these last foothills of the Alps gave rise to endless romantic tales. The area is bounded by three rivers in addition to the Danube: Triesting, Gölsen and Traisen.

Heiligenkreuz Abbey

The Cistercian abbey of Heiligenkreuz southwest of Vienna was founded by Burgundian monks on behalf of Leopold III of Babenberg in the 12th century. It was named for what is believed to be a piece of the True Cross, brought back from the Holy Land. The **Plague Column** (Pestsäule) in the courtyard and the skilfully carved choir stalls are by the baroque artist Giuliani. The cloister has 300 red marble pillars.

Mayerling

Mayerling, a peaceful little market town located some 3 km (less than 2 miles) from Heiligenkreuz, achieved its claim to fame through a tragic event: On January 30, 1889, the 30-year-old Austrian Crown Prince and Archduke Rudolf and 17-year-old Hungarian countess Maria Vetsera were found dead together in the hunting lodge — their relationship had been condemned as scandalous, and Rudolf had been refused a divorce. Emperor Franz Josef had a convent built on the spot where the couple died, and Maria Vetsera was buried in the cemetery of Heiligenkreuz, while Rudolf was laid to rest in the family tomb in Vienna.

Gumpoldskirchen

South of Vienna lies Gumpoldskirchen, one of the region's most charming wine-growing villages. Be sure to visit the 16th-century **Rathaus**, the Gothic **Michaelskirche** and local inns offering the new wine, "Heuriger".

Wien-Freudenau

Just before confluence of the Danube Canal, the Danube vessels pass the Wien-Freudenau Locks, opened in 1997, at km 1921. A much greater energy-creation project was planned further downstream in the 1980s. This would have flooded the riverbanks and destroyed the woodlands with their abundant wildlife and flora. In 1984 thousands of naturelovers protested and, since 1996, they have succeeded in protecting the last 40 km (25 miles) of the natural incline of the Danube. This stretch reaches as far as the mouth of the Morava River and has become the **Danube-Auen National Park**, one of the largest remaining floodplains of the Danube in Middle Europe.

Petronell-Carnuntum

Some 2,000 years ago, in the region of Petronell-Carnuntum (km 1890), the Roman fort of Carnuntum was built on a site overlooking the Danube, at the frontier of the Roman Empire near the crossroads of ancient European trade routes.

Petronell-Carnuntum was also conveniently sited for the Romans to go to the sulphur baths of what is today **Bad Deutsch-Altenburg** (km 1887) on the Hundsheim mountainside.

Hainburg

Hainburg (km 1884) likes to call itself Haydn-Stadt because the great composer went to school here. Medieval castle ruins and town gates recall Hainburg's former significance at the crossroads of trade routes. The narrow passage at the Danube is known as **Devín Gate** or Hainburger Pforte in German, and shortly after it, on the left bank, is the mouth of the **Morava River** (km 1880), flowing from a deep valley to mark the Austro-Slovak border. For thousands of years this gateway to the Carpathian mountains was a source of constant conflict. Both rivers were guarded by the **Devín Castle** from the time of the Celts to the 17th century. The ruin on the Slovak side is one of the Danube's most picturesque. The present day border, since 2004 an interior frontier of the EU, continues 7 km (4 miles) from the confluence downstream on the Danube and turns off to the south.

Friedensreich Hundertwasser (1928–2000). Born Christened Friedrich Stowasser, he altered his name to Friedensreich Hundertwasser ("Rich in Peace Hundredwater") in 1949, after three months at Vienna's Academy of Fine Arts—his only formal artistic training. Taking his inspiration from nature, the changing patterns reflected in water, the rhythms of Arabic music, he favoured the use of vibrant, saturated primary colours, and was particularly fascinated by the spiral. His aversion for regular, planned architecture with strict, straight lines led him to design buildings topped with trees and houses with grass roofs, uneven floors and curving walls.

Renata Holzbachová

Perched above the Danube, Bratislava Castle dominates the skyline.

Bratislava to Mohács

The new Danube–Oder canal links Bratislava to trade with Poland and eastern Germany. Today its textile, chemical, oil and metal industries are offset by pleasant forests, vineyards and farmland surrounding a handsome baroque city centre.

Bratislava

Capital of Slovakia, Bratislava (around 415,000 inhabitants), commands a key position close to Austria and Hungary. Towering over it is the royal castle. The German Pressburg, Hungarian Pozsony and Slovakian Bratislava are in fact one and the same place, its successive names testifying to a rich and varied past.

The "Little Pressburger", an antique red tourist train, takes visitors across the city's main squares and attractions.

Castle (Hrad)

Visible from afar, this majestic building with its four corner towers stands prominently on a hill above the Danube. The fortress dates back to the 9th century, but alterations took place in the 17th and 18th centuries and it is now largely Renaissance in style. It was destroyed by fire in 1811 and rebuilt only after 1953. Those rooms accessible to the public hold part of the collections of the Slovak National Museum, the Treasury and an exhibition which illustrates the history of the castle and of Slovakia and the music museum. The Castle Gardens offer a breathtaking view of the Old Quarter and the Danube.

Old Quarter

Leave the gardens by the Gothic Sigismund Gate and descend the Castle Steps to the Old Quarter. Zidovská Street boasts the finest rococo building in the city: the narrow House of the Good Shepherd, where you'll find an interesting clock museum.

St Martin's Cathedral

Diagonally opposite on the expressway (use the subway!), you'll see the 14th-century St Martin's Cathedral, one of the most beautiful examples of Gothic architecture in the whole of Slovakia. Between 1563 and 1830, 11 Hungarian monarchs and their consorts were crowned here, a fact commemorated by the golden crown topping the spire.

Main Square (Hlavné námestie)

From the cathedral, take the pretty route along Panská Street, lined with neat Renaissance and baroque palaces, to the Main Square. Of particular interest is the Old Town Hall (1325) on the eastern side. The building houses the City Museum (Mestské Múzeum).

Primate's Palace

The neoclassical Primate's Palace (Primaciálny palác) was built at the end of the 18th century. In its Mirror Hall, Napoleon and Emperor Franz I of Austria signed the Treaty of Pressburg (1805) after the crushing French victory at the Battle of Austerlitz. Part of the art collection of the City Gallery can be found here.

St Michael's Gate

Heading west, you come to St Michael's Gate, part of the former fortifications of the city. The tower, now 51 m high, has grown since it was first built at the beginning of the 14th century. In 1758 the tower was crowned with a baroque cupola, upon which St Michael sits enthroned. From the top, you have a fine view of the old town.

Reduta Palace

The Reduta Palace, renovated in 2012, is the home of the Slovak Philharmonic Orchestra. Operas and concerts are performed here.

Other Landmarks

Major theatres and museums are grouped in the elegant district between the Danube and the greenery of Hviezdoslavovo Square. At its eastern end stands the **Slovak National Theatre**, built in 1886 in neo-Renaissance style. An impressive extension, built in 2007, stands beside the Danube. The Old Bridge, **Starý most**, is being replaced by a modern one, due to be built in the new **Eurovea** quarter by 2015.

On the bank of the Danube you'll find the **National Gallery** and the **National Museum** displaying botanical and mineralogical exhibits.

Danube Bridge (Nový Most)

The modern cable-stayed Danube bridge is surmounted by a single 86-m column with a panoramic restaurant on top.

Gabčikovo Canal

The Danube flows only 23 km (14 miles) through Slovakia between Austria and Hungary before serving, from km 1850, as the Slovak-Hungarian frontier river. Then, however, for a stretch of 38 km (23.6 miles), the Danube ships leave the main river just beyond Bratislava at km 1853 to navigate the Gabčikovo Canal, 500 m wide and protected on both sides by tall dikes, flowing through Slovak territory. On a spur of land at Čunovo, where canal and river part, you sail past art works—an open-air exhibition of sculptures from the modern **Danubiana Meulensteen Art Museum**, a circular building also to be seen on the river bank.

Two smaller arms of the Danube create giant island landscapes in the plain on either side of the main river and the canal. In the north, the **Malý Dunaj** (Little Danube) embraces the 80 km (50 miles) long Žitný ostrov (Big Debris Island) on Slovak territory; in the south on Hungarian territory, the Moson-Duna (Mosoni-Danube) flows around the 50 km long Szigetköz (Small Debris Island). The many serpentine river branches and dead arms of the river with their woody marshland shelter a significant amount of birdlife.

Oops! Watch your step! (artwork in Bratislava).

Some 28 km (17 miles) further on, the canal water is dammed at the Gabčikovo hydroelectric plant. Slovakia produces here about one tenth of its electrical energy needs. Providing a height of fall of over 20 m, the second-highest locks on the Danube were opened here in 1992. The regulation of the Danube at this point protects the hinterland from flooding and guarantees controlled water levels for ship traffic. As more than three-quarters of the Danube water flows here through the canal, the rest of the Danube lowlands suffer occasionally from a water shortage, threatening gradually to dry out extensive natural woodland marshes. Some 10 km (6 miles) downstream, the canal joins the main river again at km 1811.

istockphoto.com/Brown

istockphoto.com/Sedivec

Frédérique Fasser

Road Bridges

Three distinctive road bridges across the Danube, built in different historical periods, link the Slovak left bank with the Hungarian right bank.

At km 1806, the **Vámosszabadi híd** (bridge) leads 12 km (7.5 miles) south to the old bishopric of **Győr**, formerly Raab under the Austro-Hungarian Empire. With the break-up of the Győr county, the pretty little towns of **Komárno** on the Slovak side and **Komárom** on the Hungarian side (km 1768) were created in 1920. Massive fortifications on both sides of the Danube recall the fear of Turkish attacks in the 16th and 17th century and remain the chief sights to be seen in both towns.

The **Mária Valéria Bridge** (most Márie Valérie) between the Slovakian town of Stúrovo and Esztergom (km 1719) is an expression of the new European *rapprochement*. It was first built in 1895 and named after Archduchess Marie Valerie of Austria (1868–1924). After its destruction by German troops in World War II (1944), a firm link between the Slovak and Hungarian towns was re-established only in 2001.

Basilica of Esztergom. | **Time-faded splendour on the Danube bank at Esztergom.** | **Embroidered costumes are worn for folklore shows.**

Gödöllő. Some 30 km (18.6 miles) northeast of Budapest, the town of Gödöllő is particularly well-known for its huge and handsome baroque castle. It was built from 1744 to 1748 by by Andreas Mayerhoffer for Count Antal Grassalkovich I (1694–1771). In 1867, when the emperor Franz Joseph I of Austria and his wife Elisabeth (Sissi) were crowned King and Queen of Hungary, they received it as a wedding gift. The royal pair's regular visits gave the region a new significance. The empress came often, delighted to escape from the stiff etiquette of Vienna and to practise her favourite sport, horse riding. After her death a memorial park was built.

The castle was renovated and opened to the public in 1997. Tours include the state rooms, the park and the stables.

istockphoto.com/Lane

Esztergom

Some 150 km (93 miles) southeast of Bratislava, Esztergom (km 1718), was Hungary's first capital and royal seat under the Árpád kings. King Stephen was born here around 970, and founded the cathedral in 1010. The monarchy moved out after the Mongol invasions of the 13th century, but the archbishops stayed on, taking over the royal residence. Esztergom was to pay for its ecclesiastical importance in 1543, when it was destroyed by the Turks. The restoration needed was so extensive that the Church only moved back again in 1820. Despite its clergy facing brutal persecution by the Communist authorities in the 1950s and 60s, the city has remained the centre of Hungarian Catholicism.

Basilica

The gigantic neoclassical basilica that towers over the city skyline is on the site of King Stephen's original cathedral. Begun in 1822, it took nearly 40 years to complete. The dome is based on St Peter's in Rome.

The most outstanding feature of the voluminous interior is the **Bakócz Chapel**, built in red marble by Florentine Renaissance craftsmen in the early 16th century. It's the only part of the old cathedral left.

The **Treasury** contains a magnificent collection of textiles and medieval gold relics, including the 13th-century Coronation Cross used by Hungary's kings to pledge their oaths up to the last coronation—Karl IV—in 1916. In the crypt is the tomb of Cardinal József Mindszenty, who opposed the Communist takeover after the war and was arrested and tortured. Released during the 1956 Uprising, he took refuge in the US Embassy for 15 years. He died in exile in 1975 and was reburied here with a state funeral in 1991.

Castle Museum

Located at the southern end of Castle Hill, the museum incorporates parts of the Royal Palace, including a 12th-century chapel and medieval Hall of Virtues, named after its frescoes.

Viziv, ...

Viziv); ...

Viziváros

Below Castle Hill are the attractive baroque streets of Viziváros, or Watertown district.

The beautiful **Parish Church** in the centre of Viziváros dates from 1738 and is in Italianate baroque style.

In the old Primate's Palace, the interesting **Christian Museum** (Keresztény Múzeum) houses what ranks as Hungary's greatest collection of religious art, with Italian prints, Renaissance paintings and the ornate 15th-century Garamszentbenedek coffin.

Danube-Ipoly National Park

Just beyond Esztergom, the Danube forces its way between mountainsides soaring 300 and 400 m high, in places over 900 m, of the volcanic Börzsöny mountains in the north and the Visegrád

range in the south, a stretch of river with glorious views over wooded hills and centuries-old little towns and castles. From km 1708, at the Danube's confluence on the left bank with the Slovak-Hungarian frontier river Ipoly (Ipeľ in Slovak), is the splendid landscape that is part of the National Park. With luck, you may even spot the rare Saker falcon or Short-toed snake-eagle *(Circaetus gallicus)*, which breed in these parts.

Danube Bend

At the Danube Bend (around km 1690) the river makes a right-angle turn, from heading roughly, to almost due south. Wooded hills on either side give way here and there to charming towns and villages dotted along the river banks.

The small castle town of Visegrád dominates the Danube Bend.

Visegrád

The banks of the Danube provide an idyllic setting for the remains of King Matthias Corvinus's opulent 15th-century palace at Visegrád (km 1695). Much of the sprawling residence—terraced into five levels on the hillside—has been restored.

The monumental **Hercules Fountain**, by Giovanni Dalmata, is a fine example of Hungarian Renaissance; the **Court of Honour** has graceful arcades.

Vác

Vác (km 1680) has a pretty baroque centre, its houses still painted green, red and ochre, compensating for the textile factories and cement works on the outskirts. The 18th-century cathedral has remarkable frescoes by Franz Anton Maulpertsch, while the Triumphal Arch (1764) was built specially for a visit by Queen Maria Theresa.

Szentendre

The tourist capital of the Danube Bend is the captivating town of Szentendre (km 1667). Its character has remained frozen in the 18th century. Szentendre's main square, **Fő tér**, perfectly embodies the town's spirit and history.

The towers of seven churches dominate the Szentendre skyline. The one facing Fő tér, mid-18th-century Baroque, is the Serbian Orthodox **Blagovesztenszka Church**. See also **St János Roman Catholic Parish Church** (Keresztelő Szent János-plébániatemplom) and the **Belgrade Cathedral**, an 18th-century Serbian Orthodox church noted for a richly sculpted iconastasis. Nearby is the **Serbian Orthodox Museum**, with precious icons, carvings and manuscripts. Behind the square's east side, an alley leads to the **Margit Kovács Museum** (Vastagh György 1). Kovács, who died in 1977, created stylized, elongated sculptures.

Skanzen

About 3 km (2 miles) northwest of Szentendre, typical old houses transplanted from the countryside have been assembled at the Skanzen, an open air village museum.

Szentendre Island

Beyond Visegrád, the Danube forms the 31-km long Szentendre *sziget*, a popular excursion-spot that continues as far as Budapest. Big ships sail along its east side.

Taking the Waters. You can't have everything. Hungary, occupying only one per cent of the area of Europe, lacks two significant geographical features: mountains to inspire skiers, and a seacoast. The landlocked country has to make do with the Danube and central Europe's biggest lake, **Balaton**. Bathing in Lake Balaton, which is rich in calcium and magnesium, is said to be good for you. The water is pleasantly warm, and your feet sink into the soft, sandy bottom, raising clouds of sand. It's certainly good for the fish: some of the pike-perch grow to 10 kg.

Any Hungarians not swimming in the Danube or Balaton are probably immersed in thermal baths. There are about 500 hot springs around the country, much appreciated since the time of the ancient Romans. Soaking in the spa waters — or drinking them — is supposed to cure just about any ailment you can imagine.

VISA/Louvet

Budapest
The "Paris of the East" (km 1648), is inhabited by 1.7 million people. The best place to start visiting the city is in Buda, the area to the west of the Danube. Pest, to the east, is the more modern part.

Buda
The imposing castle is reached via a **funicular** *(sikló)* linking the western side of the **Chain Bridge** to the top of Castle Hill. The funicular provides one of the most scenic rides in Budapest, and was inaugurated in 1870, when it was certainly driven by steam. It was modernised and electrified in 1986.

Castle District
Buda's fascinating zone of cobbled streets and medieval courtyards hovers over the rest of Budapest on a narrow plateau, and is protected by UNESCO. Towering above the old town is the neo-Gothic spire of the **Matthias Church**, founded in the 13th century. The building itself is essentially 19th-century neo-Gothic, attached to what the Turks left of the original edifice in 1686. Nearby rises a white rampart with gargoyles and cloisters: the **Fisherman's Bastion**. Built on the site of a medieval fish market, it recalls the fact that in the 18th century local fishermen were responsible for defending the fortifications. The present structure dates from the 20th century.

The Royal Palace
The Royal Palace was begun in the 13th century by Béla IV. After a long and turbulent history, the Royal Palace was restored to its former splendour and offers a delightful view over Pest and the Danube from its walls.

In addition to the National Library, the building houses two excellent museums. In the baroque south wing, the **Budapest History Museum** evokes the city's evolution since the Bronze Age. Downstairs in the excavated part of the medieval castle you can see the Gothic Royal Chapel of Matthias I and the Knights' Hall. On the ground floor is a roomful of striking Gothic statues unearthed in 1974.

The **Hungarian National Gallery** displays an impressive modern exhibition of Hungarian art from the Middle Ages to the present day. The entrance leads from the terrace overlooking the Danube. Among the most remarkable works, look for the splendid Late Gothic high altars, so delicately carved they look like gold lace.

Gellért Hill
The hill takes its name from an Italian missionary (Gerard or Gerardo) who converted the Hungarians but was eventually thrown from the hill in a barrel spiked with nails, in 1046, by militant heathens. His **bronze statue** stands on the north side of the hill.

At the top of the hill, the severe-looking **Citadel** was built by the Austrians after the 1848 revolution. It served in World War II as the last stronghold of the German occupying army. Their bunker has been converted into a military wax museum, the **Panoptikum 1944**, illustrating the occupation of Budapest in 1944–45. A conspicuous modern addition to the hilltop is the Soviet-inspired **Liberty Statue**, representing a gigantic woman brandishing a palm frond.

Western Bank
Down below, riverside Buda is known as Watertown because of its thermal baths. **Rudas Gyógyfürdő** or Rudas Bath, one of the most colourful, has been in business since 1556.

A short walk north of the Chain Bridge, in Batthyány tér, the twin-towered **St Anne's Church** is one of the most striking baroque structures in the city. Designed by a Jesuit, Ignatius Pretelli, in Italian style in the mid-18th century, the interior is a dazzling drama of imposing statues and marble columns.

Continuing from the square up Fő utca, you reach another 16th-century Turkish bath, the **Király Gyógyfürdő**, with a stone dome and octagonal pool.

Pest

Across the river, Pest comprises two thirds of the city's territory. The busy streets and imposing boulevards offer plenty to see.

Danube's Eastern Shore

Along the embankment, the imposing **Hungarian Parliament Building** stands as a symbol of the grandeur of the Austro-Hungarian Empire. Excellent guided tours are available; among other splendours, you will see the royal sceptre, crown and orb, which have a long and adventurous history, having been variously buried in Transylvania and locked up in Fort Knox before being returned to Hungary in 1978.

The oldest surviving structure in Pest, nestled against the flyover leading to Elizabeth Bridge, is the **Inner City Parish Church**. Founded in the 12th century, it served some time as a mosque under the Turkish occupation; a Muslim prayer niche is still to be seen near the altar.

The cobbled centrepiece of an expansive pedestrian zone, **Váci utca** is packed with trendy boutiques and the stalls of street vendors. There are several cafés and restaurants where you can sit and

istockphoto.com/Butterfield

Huber/Schmid

Matthias Church in Buda, with its colourful tiled roof. | **A quick way up to the Royal Palace.**

The Hungarian Parliament Building seen
from Fisherman's Bastion (Halászbástya).

contemplate the street's eclectic architectural mix.

At 1 Vámház körút, the cavernous red-brick and cast-iron **Central Market Hall** is full of local colour. It was designed by Samu Pecz and opened in 1897.

Small Boulevard (Kiskörút)

Vestiges of the city's medieval walls have been attractively incorporated into more recent buildings, notably in the streets that form part of the Kiskörút or Small Boulevard.

Vámház körút and Múzeum körút intersect at Kálvin tér, where you might wish to make a foray into Üllői út to visit the distinctive building that houses the **Museum of Applied Arts**. The style of the brick-and-ceramic-tile palace is listed as Art Nouveau, though it might be described as Fantasy Hungarian with strong eastern influences. Further south, on Páva útca, the **Holocaust Memorial Center** includes a magnificently renovated synagogue, as well as a new building complex with exhibition halls, conference rooms and research centre.

The Múzeum körút section is dominated by the **Hungarian National Museum**, with a magnificent neoclassical façade. The huge exhibition is imaginatively designed and covers the nation's history, from the Stone Age to the collapse of communism.

Along Andrássy Avenue

Be sure to take a stroll along the most stately avenue in Budapest, the UNESCO listed Andrássy út, modelled after the Champs-Elysées in the 1870s. Its name has been changed many times, but by any title this remains a spacious, patrician thoroughfare.

The neo-Renaissance **State Opera House** is the most admired building on the avenue. Statues of 16 great composers stand high above the entrance, with Franz Liszt and Ferenc Erkel in places of honour.

The **House of Terror Museum** is located at no. 60. In 1944, this building was the seat of the Hungarian national-socialist party. The building has been transformed into a memorial illustrating the methods of the two 20th century reigns of terror.

Nearby, at the corner of Vörösmarty utca, is the **Liszt Ferenc Memorial Museum**, which houses the 19th-century composer's instruments, books and other personal belongings. Further on is the **Zoltán Kodály Memorial Museum and Archives**. Along with Liszt and Bartók, Kodály (1882–1967) completes Hungary's triumvirate of great composers. Here in his house you can see his book-lined study, piano, and a collection of jugs which typify his love of traditional folk art. (The museum can only be visited by appointment.)

The neo-Renaissance Opera House, with its horseshoe-shaped Auditorium, is one of Budapest's gems.

Facing each other across the expanse of Heroes' Square are two almost identical neoclassical buildings. The larger one, at the left side of the square, is the **Museum of Fine Arts** (Szepmüvészeti Múzeum). The building, built between 1900 and 1906, was designed by lbert Schickedanz and Fülöp Herczog. Its comprehensive collection of paintings, including a number by French Impressionists, makes it an institution of international importance.

The smaller clone, the **Kunst-halle** (Műcsarnok) or Palace of Arts, houses eclectic temporary exhibitions of paintings by Hungarian and foreign artists. Established in the 19th century, the museum was built by the same architects who designed the Museum of Fine Arts.

Heroes' Square

Andrássy avenue ends with a flourish at the vast and airy Heroes' Square (Hősök tere), with the **Millennium Memorial** as its centrepiece, topped by a statue of the archangel Gabriel. Begun on the thousandth anniversary of the Magyar conquest, the monument depicts Prince Árpád and his chieftains enclosed in a colonnade of Hungary's most illustrious leaders, ranging from King Stephen I to Kossuth, the 1848 revolutionary.

Városliget (City Park)

The vast City Park, accessed from the Heroes' Square, sprawls beyond the Millenium Memorial. Among its amenities are an artificial lake, a municipal zoo, an amuseument park and the extraordinary **Castle of Vajdahunyad**, modelled on a Transylvanian castle.

The castle houses the interesting **Hungarian Agricultural Museum** (Mezőgazdasági Múzeum), the biggest agricultural museum in Europe.

In front of the Hungarian Museum sits the hooded statue of a royal scribe known only as **Anonymous**, who wrote the first Hungarian chronicles. The figure of George Washington was presented to Budapest in 1906 by Hungarian settlers in the United States.

Széchenyi Baths

Across from the park is the triple dome of the Széchenyi Baths. First built in 1913, this was one of Europe's largest medicinal bath complexes. The amusing sight of people playing chess while soaking in the healing waters is not to be missed.

From Budapest to Kalocsa

On this stretch, the Danube is bordered by dense shrubbery and trees. For the first 100 km south of Budapest, villages are more frequently seen than in the flat country on the left bank.

Dunaújváros

The steel centre of Dunaújváros (km 1578), designed in the 1950s, was built on the site of the Roman military base of Intercisum. The **Intercisa Museum** is devoted to the Roman fortifications. Since 2007, a highway bridge spans from the Danube to Dunavecse.

The Puszta. Also known as the Great Plain, the vast, flat prairie of the Puszta was Hungary's very own Wild West during the 19th century, when huge herds of cattle grazed here watched over by cowboys, called *gulyás*. It was once covered in thick forest, but was laid waste during the Turkish occupation, because of the invaders' need for timber to build fortresses. Its renaissance as pastureland was due to the irrigation works on the River Tisza in the early 19th century. By the 20th century, the success of the irrigation scheme meant it could sustain crop development, and big landowners carried out wholesale enclosure, killing off the cattle industry and creating widespread poverty among the peasants. Under post-war communism, the estates were nationalized, and huge collective farms introduced, only to be broken up after 1989 and returned to private ownership. Today, you will find pleasant little towns beyond which are attractive old whitewashed farmsteads adorned with bright-coloured strings of paprika. In 1999, the cultural landscape of the Puszta, represented by the **Hortobágy National Park**—the largest semi-natural grassland in Europe—was inscribed on the UNESCO World Heritage list.

Marguerite Martinoli

Dunaföldvár
Dunaföldvár (km 1560), where a road and rail bridge spans the Danube, recalls the era of Turkish invasions with its Turkish bastion and the castle museum.

Harta
Harta (km 1546) on the left bank dates back to Swabian (German) settlers brought here by Austria's Archduchess Maria Theresa in the 18th century.

Paks
The major attractions of Paks (km 1531) are the outstanding Catholic **Church of the Holy Ghost** designed by Imre Makovecz and its renowned fish-soup, as well as the country's only nuclear power station south of town (km 1526).

Kiskunság National Park
In the sandy highlands between the Danube and the Tisza, the Kiskunság National Park (530 sq km, over 200 sq miles) comprising nine separate areas, preserves for posterity the historical landscapes of the Puszta and important nature reserves. Most of them have been declared UNESCO Biosphere Reserves. You will come across the region's typical domestic and pasturing animals as well as rare bird species such as spoonbills, purple herons and silver herons.

Kalocsa
The farming town of Kalocsa (km 1516) has something for every taste—history, folklore, art, and one of Europe's most offbeat museums. Kalocsa was founded in the 11th century alongside the Danube, but the river subsequently changed its mood and its course, leaving the town 6 km (3.7 miles) from the nearest fish or boat. Happily, the newly enlarged boundaries of Kalocsa included fertile meadows, where fruit and vegetables and grain grow. The dominant crop, though, is red paprika—the so-called "red gold".

Holy Trinity Square
Kalocsa's Szentháromság tér features statues of two national heroes—King (Saint) Stephen and Franz (Ferenc in Hungarian) Liszt. The 18th-century **Cathedral**, in graceful baroque style, stands on the site of a series of churches, going back to the 11th century.

In the **Archbishop's Palace** across the square, the library contains over 100,000 volumes, including a Bible autographed by Martin Luther.

Museums
In the **Paprika Museum** you can follow the saga of the Mexican hot pepper through its Hungarian naturalisation.

In the **Viski Károly Museum** (István király utca 25) are displays of traditional farm tools, antique furniture and decorations.

A master of kinetic art, Nicolas Schöffer (1912–92) donated some of his works to his home town; they are displayed in his house of birth, now the **Nicolas Schöffer Collection**, at Szent István Király út 76—the same street as the Viski Károly Museum.

Run by the Kalocsa Folk Art Cooperative, the **House of Folk Arts** displays antique agricultural implements and rustic furnishings. Kalocsa embroidery is on show—and on sale—and they stage folklore exhibitions in which the local youngsters dance to typically vivacious Hungarian music.

East of Kalocsa

The pleasant cities of **Kecskemét** and **Szeged**, two important regional centres, are well worth a visit. Along the way you can make a stop at a traditional *csárda*, or wayside inn, serving rustic food.

Sió Valley

Just beyond a modern motorway bridge (km 1499) spanning the now slowly flowing Danube, surrounded mostly by lush marshy woodland, is the confluence with the River Sió, transformed here into a canal for its 123-km course from **Lake Balaton**, plied by pleasure boats and ships.

Szekszárd

Above the Sió Valley, 15 km (9 miles) west of the Danube, Szekszárd is the centre of a wine-growing region. The county seat, it has a high proportion of citizens of German and Serbian descent. Their pedigree can be traced back to the 150 years of Turkish occupation, when Szekszárd was a ghost town. To renew the population in the 18th century, settlers from neighbouring countries were welcomed. Local history starts in the 11th century, when King Béla I founded a fortified Benedictine monastery on a hill. The courtyard of the present County Hall is built around the remains of an ancient chapel and the abbey church.

Baja

Along a stretch of the Danube surrounded by virgin forests as far as Baja (km 1479), you reach the southernmost Hungarian bridge on the Danube, Türr István híd. Over this vital link between east and west Hungary carries rail traffic as well as cars and trucks (eastbound and west-bound alternate), all on a single lane. Long before there was a bridge, the Turkish invaders, aware of the strategic significance, fortified the town. Today the enormous main square, Szentháromság tér, gives an idea of the historic importance of Baja.

Danube-Drava National Park

From the lower reaches of the Sió in the north to Hungary's southern border, the Danube-Drava National Park covers a surface of 500 sq km (193 sq miles) through which the Danube flows for 65 km (40 miles) as well as a portion of its Drava tributary.

Across the sometimes narrow, sometimes several kilometres wide floodplain with often impenetrable forest, countless tributary streams, dead arms of the river and stagnant pools form a landscape constantly changing with the considerable seasonal variations in water levels.

Danube travellers make their way for hours through this wild landscape of water, woods and islands along the meandering branches of the main river. White egrets and grey herons, cormorants and wild ducks throng the banks, osprey and black stork breed on the reserve.

Gemenc Forest

This northwest area of the Danube-Drava National Park was included in the main park in 1996. Nature lovers can explore the forest along nature trails via a narrow-gauge railway and on boat tours. Besides rare birds, they may also spot deer, stag, beaver and wild boar.

Mohács

The Danube port city of Mohács (km 1447) is forever linked with a melancholy chapter in Hungarian history. It unfolded swiftly, a few kilometres out of town, on August 29, 1526. A well-equipped army of Sultan Suleiman the Magnificent, with a four-to-one advantage in manpower, crushed the defending forces of the Hungarian King Louis (Lajos) II. The king died during the retreat. For the next century and a half Hungary endured Ottoman occupation. The modern **Votive Church** (Fogadalmi Templom) in the centre of town is one of the local memorials to these events. Meant to give thanks for the eventual expulsion of the Turks, it might be mistaken for a mosque, but for the dome topped by a big cross.

On the actual site of the battle, a **Memorial Park** is strewn with haunting modern sculptures symbolising the opposing forces. The ghosts of the generals, the soldiers and the horses—in imaginative wood-carvings—are forever deployed across the field of battle. The park was dedicated in 1976 on the 450th anniversary of an unforgettable defeat.

The people of Mohács celebrate the departure of the Turks at Carnival time, when they parade in the scariest giant masks. The Busó carnival also aims to expel another invader—winter.

PÉCS

On the southern slopes of the Mecsek hills, west of Mohács, 200 km south of Budapest, the university town of Pécs (population 158,000) is the largest city in Transdanubia. Chosen as European Capital of Culture in 2010, the city is being rejuvenated, and the historic core carefully restored. On the ancient trade route from the German-speaking countries to the Balkans and Middle East, Pécs unites cultures of east, west and south.

You will see traces left behind by the former inhabitants—Celts, Romans, Turks, Germans and Hungarians. In Roman times, Hadrian called the town Sopianae and made it the capital of Pannonia. Some parts of the **Roman aqueduct** can still be seen, and the Early Christian **Necropolis**, listed as a UNESCO World Heritage Site in 2000, is composed of a remarkable series of decorated tombs. Many fine relics of prehistoric and Roman times are displayed in the **Archaeological Museum** (Széchenyi tér 12).

The Hungarians conquered the area in the late 9th century and their king Stephen (István, 997–1038) made Pécs an ecclesiastical centre.

King Matthias built the circular, crenellated **Barbacan**, a gate tower for the castle. It stands next to the Bishops' Palace. After the Battle of Mohács in 1526, the Ottoman army invaded Pécs. The city was occupied by the Turks from 1543. Churches were turned into mosques, Turkish baths and minarets were built, and a bazaar replaced the market. The Turks also introduced new kinds of grapes, among them *kadarka*.

After the expulsion of the Turks, Pécs became part of the Habsburg Empire. The large **Mosque of Pasha Qasim** has been transformed into the parish church. It stands at the top of Széchenyi tér. The high round dome and striped arches remain from the Muslim era, but the congregation is now Hungarian and Catholic; a crucifix stands over the prayer niche. A marble tablet inscribed in elegant Arabic calligraphy spells out a verse of the Koran translated into Hungarian.

On Rákóczi út, another mosque, **Pasha Hassan Yakovali**, is still a place of Muslim worship and a small museum displaying Turkish armour, stirrups, rugs, pottery and utensils; it is the only mosque in Hungary whose minaret is intact.

From the early 18th century, under the Habsburgs, the city flourished. Queen Maria Theresa granted Pécs the status of a free royal town. The architecture of many grand residences and public bulding in ornate baroque style dates back to this period.

Peter and Paul Cathedral, built over a 4th century church, was reworked in the 19th century in the Tuscan Romanesque style. In Roman times, the area was the centre of a cemetery and many early Christian burial vaults have been excavated nearby.

Industry continued to develop in the second half of the 19th century: iron foundries, paper-makers, sugar-refineries and coal-mining were significant, and the Zsolnay Porcelain works were established in 1853. Zsolnay majolica adorns many of the town house façades, as well as the famous **Zsolnay Fountain** on Széchenyi tér. The **Zsolnay Museum** (Káptalan utca 2) offers an overview of the history of the factory. The 1869 **Synagogue**, on Goldmark Károly utca, bears a plaque honouring the local victims of Auschwitz.

By the early 20th century, Pécs had developed to become one of Hungary's biggest towns. Its citizens built Eclectic-style houses, a splendid **National Theatre** on Kossuth Lajos utca, a

David Warden

The porcelain bull's heads decorating the Zsolnay Fountain have a metallic sheen.

fine **Town Hall** and an ornate **Railway Station**. The only Art Nouveau building in the city, the main **Post Office** on Jókai utca, bears witness to this period.

One of Pécs' famous sons was Victor Vasarely (1906–1997); many of his works are displayed in the **Vasarely Museum** on Káptalan utca. The **Csontváry Museum** (11 Janus Pannonius utca) displays the great naive painter's works.

The **Modern Hungarian Gallery** has displays in two separate locations: 5 Papnövelde utca and 4 Káptalan utca.

A skein of birds flies over the reserve of Kopački Rit, between Danube and Drava.

Kroatische Zentrale für Tourismus

Downriver to Belgrade

After leaving Hungary at km 1433, the Danube serves for about 137 km (85 miles) as a frontier (still disputed) between Croatia and Serbia, and is no longer called Duna, but Dunav.

Bezdan

A bridge (km 1425) links the hillside Croatian village of Batina with the little Serbian town of Bezdan, 5 km away. This is the western end of the canal network started in the early 19th century—and frequently expanded—between the Danube and Tisza. The historic locks designed by Gustave Eiffel in 1880 on the 123-km **Veliki-Bački Canal** to the Tisza is, like many other sections of the artificial network of waterways, no longer practicable for modern commercial shipping.

Bačka

The Bačka, a fertile plain bound by the Danube to the west and south and the Tisza to the east, is divided between Hungary and Serbia. Its southern border is marked by Novi Sad, the capital of Vojvodina. The Bačka was settled by Swabians from Germany (usually referred to as Danube Swabians) after the Turks were driven out in the 17th and 18th centuries.

Apatin

Apatin (km 1401), located in the north-western part of the Bačka, was founded by German settlers in the 18th century. The town became famous for its hemp ropes and beer and even today the view over the Serbian town is dominated by the gigantic silos of the Jelen brewery. Now only a small proportion of the population is German-speaking.

Kopački Rit Nature Park

The extensive floodplain landscape of the **River Drava**'s confluence region is very much in evidence right here on the Croatian bank. The river has its source in the Alps and raises its water level considerably after the snow thaw and autumn rains. The Kopački Rit Nature Park located in the wedge of land between the Danube and Drava is a 239 sq-km Eldorado for fish and one of the most important bird sanctuaries in Europe. Tens of thousands of migratory birds spend their winter here, among them the rare greater spotted eagle, while the black stork and white-tailed sea eagle rear their young here. The Danube winds its way as far as the mouth of the Drava (km 1383) and beyond in many curves with greatly increased water volume. Islands, lateral branches of the river and shallows complicate the ships' passage.

The red rooftops of the pretty baroque city of Osijek by the Drava.

Osijek

The most important town in the region of Slavonia at the eastern edge of Croatia, Osijek lies 20 km upstream on the Drava and has around 110,000 inhabitants. In the course of history, Illyrians, Romans, Hungarians and Slavs lived here by the river. The Turks built a wooden bridge over the Drava with a fortress which the Habsburgs later transformed into a baroque stronghold (Croatian Tvrđa). Town life, brightened up by its university students, is focused in the Lower Town (*donj*

grad) to the east of the citadel. Further upstream, Europska Avenija is lined with ornate historical buildings in Art Nouveau and Vienna Secession style.

On the skyline looms the tower of the neo-Gothic **co-cathedral of Peter and Paul** (1898), located in the Upper Town (*gornji grad*). The man who initiated its construction was Bishop Josip Jurak Strossmayer (1819–1905), born in Osijek and politically very active for the Croatian cause from his diocese in Đakovo.

Đakovo

In this little town some 60 km (37 miles) to the south, the outstanding monument is the huge neo-Romanesque and neo-Gothic **Cathedral of St Peter**, built 1888–82 and Strossmayer's burial place. This rustic centre is known for its annual embroidery folklore festival in July and for its 500-year-old stud farm. For 200 years it has specialized in the breeding of Lipizzaners (stars of Vienna's Spanish Riding School), trained here as coach-horses.

Vukovar

The port of Vukovar (km 1333) serves as a gateway for excursions into Croatia's fertile rural region west of the Danube. With its churches, patrician houses and arcaded passages near the 18th-century **Eltz Manor**, the baroque castle of the counts of Eltz, Vukovar was once regarded as a jewel of urban baroque architecture. In 1991, it fell victim to the Battle of Vukovar, fought during the Croatian War of Independence (1991–1995). After Serbian-occupied eastern Slavonia was restored to Croatia in 1998, reconstruction began in earnest.

Construction of new buildings and restoration of historical edifices such as the **Franciscan Monastery**, one of the oldest baroque monuments in Vukovar, offer hope for a renaissance of the most important Croatian port town on the Danube. Visible from the river, the bullet-riddled **Water Tower**, destroyed by the Serbian forces, makes a sad yet important historical landmark.

Rain Dance. The Indians of North America are not the only ones who perform dances to pray for rain: similar customs have also been known on the Danube. In Serbia's Bačka Palanka, men and women would dance at the harvest festival, douse each other with water and sing for the heavens to open. A group of girls would proceed through the village, their leader clad only in flowers, grass and leaves, to be greeted from each threshold with a bucketful of water.

Ilok

The Srijem landscape, where Romans introduced vineyards, extends past the little Croatian town of Ilok (km 1299). The hill close to the river bank makes an ideal lookout, site of the medieval fortification protected by a town wall of bricks. The restored church tower of the 18th-century **Franciscan Monastery** juts out as a last bastion of predominantly Catholic Croatia. Ilok's main attraction is the **City Museum**, located in the baroque Odescalchi Palace. The **Ilok–Bačka Palanka Bridge** (km 1297) links Ilok with the Serbian town of Bačka Palanka, an important agricultural centre.

Bačka Palanka

Bačka Palanka is worth a visit for its Serbian Orthodox **Church of St John the Baptist** (1783), one of the oldest churches of Vojvodina. From km 1296, the Danube flows for 221 km through Serbia.

Fruška Gora

In the hinterland behind the right bank are the wooded hills of Fruška Gora, a low island mountain with grapes and plums growing on the slopes. Far away in the hills, over a dozen Orthodox monasteries lie hidden, mostly built in the 16th century. A national park covers 250 sq km of these hills, but only a small part on its western side belongs to Croatia.

Novi Sad

At km 1255, this is the principal town of Vojvodina, the granary of former Yugoslavia. Founded at the end of the 17th century by Serbs fleeing from the Turks, Novi Sad was declared a royal free city in 1748. A century later the Hungarians virtually razed it to the ground. In the 19th century the town was a cultural and intellectual focus for the Serbs within the Austro-Hungarian empire, when it became known as (yet another) Athens of the North. Nowadays, the city has an urban population of over 250,000.

Architecturally, Novi Sad offers little of interest, but it does have the **Museum of Vojvodina**, dedicated to art and natural history, and the **Museum of Contemporary Art of Vojvodina** with an extensive collection of paintings. Additionally, lively festivals and cultural events are organised all year round.

In 1999 the three bridges of Novi Sad were destroyed by NATO bombs; since then they have all been replaced. The last and most modern, the **Liberty Bridge** (Most slobode), was completed in 2005.

Orthodox saints in the monastery of Novo Hopovo, Fruška Gora. | A welcome thirst-quencher. | The fortress of Petrovaradin overlooks Novi Sad. | The attractive spires of Sremski Karlovci.

THE TISZA

Originating in the Carpathian mountains of western Ukraine, the Tisza winds slowly through Hungary southwards and links up with the Danube in Serbia, just north of Belgrade. It actually flows longer inside Hungary than the Danube. Notorious for flooding, it has been improved by the construction of thousands of kilometres of embankments, straightened out in places and harnessed to provide hydro-electric power and irrigation. The best-known cities along its shores are Tokaj, in the northeast region of Hungary, and Szeged in the south. Tokaj is known for its fine wines and Szeged for spicy salami and a highly seasoned fish soup.

Tokaj lies at the spot where the Tisza makes a 90° turn south-wards, at a conjunction with the scenic Bodrog river. Terraced vineyards cling to the hillside above town; the streets are full of wine cellars where you can taste many varieties of their sweet wines. One has been converted into a museum *(Tokaji múzeum)* documenting the ancient methods of production. In 2002, the cultural landscape of the Tokaj Wine Region was UNESCO-listed.

Szeged is a river port and cultural centre, boasting two universities which confer on the city a young and cheerful atmosphere. The layout of concentric boulevards and streets on a grid pattern was devised after a devastating flood in 1879. In the town centre on Széchenyi tér, among lawns, flower gardens and fountains, is the ornate City Hall, in what is known as Eclectic baroque style. South from here is the main shopping area, reserved for pedestrians. The great pinnacled Votive Church and Cathedral of Our Lady of Hungary, with eight clocks on its twin towers, was erected between 1913 and 1930. The Szeged Summer Festival of opera and ballet is held in the square outside. In front of the church is the sturdy medieval Tower of St Demetrius. The 18th-century Serbian Ortodox church in Dóm tér (Cathedral Square) houses a superb collection of Orthodox icons. By the river at the Palace of Education (1896), the Ferenc Morá Museum gives insight into Szeged's history and the importance of the River Tisza. The imposing New Synagogue, built in 1907, is one of the most beautiful in Europe.

Petrovaradin

Standing opposite the town on the right bank of the river, the fortress of Petrovaradin is well worth a visit. Tke a look at the clock tower: the hour hand is longer than the minute hand. Fortified by monks in the 13th century, the citadel fell to Suleiman the Magnificent three centuries later. Prince Eugene of Savoy—celebrated in folk songs as the "noble knight"—managed to drive out the Turks in 1716. The Austrians undertook construction of a new citadel, using plans drawn up by the famous French military architect Vauban. As Napoleon's armies advanced upon Vienna, the treasures of the Imperial Court were hurried to the safety of Petrovaradin. In the mid-19th century, Hungarian freedom fighters captured the fortress, but they were overcome by loyalist Croats and Serbs. For a long time afterwards the citadel served as both barracks and prison, housing such illustrious inmates as Josip Broz, later to become Marshal Tito.

Sremski Karlovci

Continuing downriver you reach Sremski Karlovci (km 1246), a pretty little town with fine baroque houses. It's famous in history as the place where the peace treaty of 1699 (the Treaty of Karlowitz) was signed by Austria, Turkey, Poland and Venice, putting an end to the war with the Turks and giving Austria supremacy in the Balkans. Apparently the room in which the treaty was signed had to be provided with four doors, as the delegations couldn't come to an agreement as to which of them was to

enter first. To return to the present, Sremski Karlovci is known for its excellent red wine (and also its rosé); the best place to sample them is right here on the spot.

Stari Slankamen

The stronghold of Stari Slankamen (km 1215) is a reminder of a battle against the Ottomans in 1691; today's visitors come for a peaceful soak in the warm, sodium-rich waters of the geothermal springs.

Zemun

Zemun (km 1173), now just a suburb of Belgrade, was founded by the Romans, who called it Taurunum. After 1526 the Turks fortified the town; later it fell to Austria, and until 1918 the Hungarian border ran past here.

Belgrade

The capital of Serbia, Belgrade (Beograd, km 1170) is one of four capital cities standing on the Danube. Along with Vienna, Bratislava and Budapest, it was a crucial site in Europe's commercial and communications network even before Roman times.

When the Roman Empire was split into East and West in 395, the seat of power moved from Rome to Constantinople. Byzantium was allotted Belgrade in its portion, and the boundary between the two parts of the empire ran beneath the city walls. The division is still mirrored in Belgrade's adherence to the Orthodox faith, which evolved throughout Byzantium. The Byzantines were not alone in coveting Belgrade. Bulgars, Hungarians, Austrians and Turks all held it over the ages.

The city was badly bombed in the two world wars of the 20th century, and because of its strategic situation, was occupied by Austria and Germany. Belgrade has been destroyed and rebuilt many times. The postwar period has seen it change from a small Balkan town to a modern European metropolis, with a population of more than 1 million, and capital of Serbia. In rebuilding, the emphasis was placed on the scientific, educational, cultural and conference infrastructures.

The country applied for membership of the EU in 2009; it received candidate status in 2012, and negotiations to join the Union started in January 2014.

Fortress

Looming over the meeting point of the Danube and the Sava is the old fortress within three sets of ramparts, watching over its upper and lower towns. The Romans built their fortifications up on the hill in the 1st century, and they were reinforced by the Byzantines several centuries later. When the Austrians occupied the fortress in 1717–39, after temporarily dis-

The sturdy old fortress of Belgrade commands respect. | Folk singers in traditional Serbian costume. | A wide and elegant stairway leads up to Kalemegdan, around the fortress.

lodging the Turks, they made it one of the mightiest bastions of all Europe. Today the citadel houses a military museum, and everything speaks of the passage of time. Within the upper walls are some ancient remains: a Roman well, a Turkish mausoleum, a corbelled building. The Turkish hammam at the foot of the hill has been converted into a planetarium. **Kalemegdan**, the area around the fortress, is now a park.

City Centre
Belgrade's lively city centre stretches to the east of the fortress. Here you'll find several interesting buildings.

Knez Mihailova Street
Running southeast of the fortress, the old Roman road to the south, Ulica Knez Mihailova, is now a protected pedestrian area. You can stroll past shops and art galleries right through to **Terazije Square**, looking up to admire the baroque, Art Nouveau and Social Realist façades.

Students' Square
Students' Square (Studentski Trg) is a central urban neighbourhood near **Studentski Park**, a favourite retreat for university students. Visit the **Ethnographic Museum** (Etnografski muzej), devoted to Serbian arts and folklore, at the park's western end.

Republic Square
In Republic Square (Trg Republike) you'll find some of the city's most distinguishable landmarks: the 19th-century building of the **National Theatre** (Narodno pozorište), an equestrian **statue of Prince Mihajlo** or Michael (1882), who played a major role in ending the Turkish occupation in the 19th century, and the **National Museum** (Narodni muzej), the oldest museum in Serbia (currently closed for renovation works).

Skadarlija
A few minutes' walk to the east of Republic Square is the old bohemian district of Skadarlija—in fact just one sloping cobbled street. Here in the evening, among the numerous small art galleries you'll come across painters, roving actors, fortune-tellers and musicians, all in a good-humoured atmosphere. The music played in the cosy restaurants and wine houses goes on until the small hours.

Varoš Kapija
Just south of the fortress is the old quarter of Varoš kapija (City Gate). Here you will find the **Museum of the Serbian Orthodox Church**, set in the Patriarch's residence houses. Opposite is the **Cathedral Church of Saint Michael the Archangel**, built in neoclassical style in 1837–40. Several reli-

gious figures and Serbian over-lords are buried beneath the altar and in the crypt, among them Prince Miloš Obrenović, one of the leaders of the second Serbian revolt against the Turks, who set a dynasty on the throne (1815–42 then 1858–1903). The same prince had a pretty white man-sion, the **Residence of Princess Ljubi-ca** (Konak kneginje Ljubice) built for his wife in 1831. Full of an-tique furniture and ornaments, its Turkish baths, oriental carpets and floor-level seating show how the Turks influenced the lifestyle of the Serbian rulers.

Around the City
Other remarkable points of inter-est lie just outside the city centre including, in a southerly direction, St Sava Cathedral and Topčider Park. Don't miss the Museum of Contemporary Art on the other side of the Sava; the river also lends itself to a pleasant cruise.

St Sava Cathedral
Looking back over the city, you can't miss the cathedral's dome, dominating the skyline from the Vračar plateau. This is the largest Orthodox church in the world, big enough to hold a congregation of 11,000. Construction began in the early 20th century and it's now mostly completed and accessible, though it will take years to finish its interior decoration.

Topčider
Further south stretches Topčider's lovely park, planted with plane trees and a central flowerbed. There are several cafés and the historic palace of Prince Milŏs.

Ada Ciganlija
This artificial island on the Sava is home to open-air sports grounds, a golf course and mod-ern Stonehenge sculptures by Ratko Vulanovic.

West of the Sava
The **Museum of Contemporary Art** is on the other side of the Sava, at Novi Beograd (New Belgrade). It's worth taking the impressive cruise at the mouth of the Sava to see the fortress watching over the city. The elegant **Ada Bridge** (2012) crosses the Danube at km 1167.

Excursions from Belgrade
One of the most popular side trips is to **Mount Avala**, 18 km (11 miles) away, with its tall telecommunica-tion tower and the Monument to the Unknown Hero. History buffs will enjoy a trip to **Topola**, perched high on **Oplenac Hill** south of Bel-grade. A fort marks the spot where the rebellion against the Turks began in 1804. Karadjordje, the leader of the uprising, is buried here in the richly decorated St George's church. The family mausoleum and King Peter's House are also worth a visit.

From Belgrade to Ram

Fed by the Drava, Tisza and Sava rivers, the Danube below Belgrade swells considerably. Citadels and fortresses are dotted along the banks.

Smederevo

The fortress of Smederevo was built by Djuradj Brankovič in 1430, only to be captured by the Ottomans in 1459. After the pipeline bridge (km 1113) to Smederevska Ada, **Kovinski most** (km 1112) is the last link across the river for 169 km. On the right bank you will see the mouth of the **Great Morava** (km 1104), the final section of the Morava. Further on, near **Kostolac** (km 1094), the **River Mlava** flows into the Danube. The town of Viminacium once stood here; it was the capital of the Roman province of Moesia Superior.

Ram

Before the start of the border with Romania lies the 16th-century **Ram Fortress** (Tvrđava Ram) (km 1077). A ferry links Ram with **Banatska Palanka**, the last Serbian town on the Danube left bank. The lower reaches of the River Nera form the border with Romania.

The elegant St Sava Cathedral in Belgrade. | Rustic gathering in the Serbian countryside. | Natural wonders are not far from the centre of Belgrade.

istockphoto.com/V. Marinkovic

Serbian National Tourist Board

Serbian National Tourist Board/D. Bosnic

The ruins of Golubac Castle, clinging to its rock.

Nationale Tourismus Organisation Serbiens / Dragan Bosnic

Downriver to Silistra

For 229 km after the city of Ram, the Danube serves as the Romanian-Serbian border and dominates the skyline of the Carpathian mountains.

Veliko Gradište

The Serbian town of Veliko Gradšte (km 1059), where lucrative copper deposits were exploited under the Roman Emperor Hadrian, is now a stopover for international shipping to undergo a border control.

Moldova Veche

Moldova Veche (km 1048), on the site of the Roman settlement of Mudava, was once an important station for shipping. Its river port is one of the largest in Romania.

The Iron Gate

Just after Moldova Veche, the river flows into a narrow defile, 130 km (80 miles) long, separating the Carpathian Mountains from the Balkans. Once feared for its rapids and cataracts, the terror of sailors in bygone days, the cataract channel was tamed by the construction of a dam and the gigantic Đerdap hydroelectric power station, inaugurated in 1971. Today, the water level is 35 m higher than before the building of the dam's weir. Some 25,000 inhabitants of 17 towns along the former course of the Danube had to be resettled. The journey through the towering mountain ranges on each side of the river, known in its last part as the Đerdap or Iron Gate, still has the power to impress voyagers.

Golubac Castle

On the right bank emerges the gloomy silhouette of Golubac castle (km 1039). Despite its ruined state, the castle, held by the Turks for 260 years, inspires respect with its nine massive towers joined by a ring of walls.

Rising steeply from the depths of the river, the infamous **Babakai Rock** has been the inspiration for many myths and legends.

Gorges

The narrow reaches of the river that follow with their steep gorges (known as *klisure*, plural of *klisura*) alternating with bays and wider stretches present not only enchanting landscapes but also historic and prehistoric landmarks.

Golubac Gorge

Along the Golubac Gorge or Golubačka klisura (km 1040–km 1026), a plaque at km 1036 commemorates Gábor Baross. As Hungarian minister of transport from 1886 to 1892, he introduced the necessary adjustments for the dangerous Danube rapids.

In the adjoining **Liubcova Basin** (km 1026–1015) are the villages of Liubcova and Berzasca. The Serbian village of **Dobra** (km 1021) is built along the narrow wooded valley of a tributary, with its picturesque cemetery located directly on the Danube river bank.

The port of **Drencova** (km 1016) was once the last stop for steamships, with passengers disembarking for smaller vessels or taking a coach to circumvent the cataracts.

Upper Klisura

Upper Klisura (or Gornja Klisura) is the name of the narrow valley that extends from km 1015 to km 999. At km 1011, a plaque (visible only when the water level is low enough) recalls the road building under Emperor Tiberius (AD 14–37) and his successors. The Roman road was hewn from the rock or ran for some stretches as a gallery formed by beams set in the rock. It was completed under Trajan (AD 98–117) but now lies submerged beneath the river's higher water level.

The famous settlement of **Lepenski Vir** (km 1004) dates back to 8000–4000 BC but was not discovered until 1965. To protect it, archaeologists transferred the buildings to higher ground on a hill above the river. The complex ground plans of the excavated buildings testify to a high level of cultural development, and the large river pebbles which were found on this spot, carved with fishlike faces, are the earliest sculptures of this sort discovered in Europe.

Lower Klisura

At the striking **Greben Rock**, which juts out at km 999, is the start of the Lower or Donja Klisura (km 999–965). The gorge soon opens into the **Milanovac Basin**, which is up to 2 km wide in places. The Romanian Sviniţa (km 995) and the Serbia **Donji Milanovac** (km 991) have been resettled at a higher altitude, while opposite, the remains of two of the **Tricule** bastion's original three towers still stand out in the river near the bank.

Ðerdap National Park

Serbia has created this unique park out of a strip of hinterland 2 to 8 km (1 to 5 miles) wide along the 103-km stretch of the Danube from the Golubac fortress to the Ðerdap 1 Hydroelectric Power Station. The park covers an area of 636 sq km (245 sq miles).

istockphoto.com/F. Kienas

Serbian National Tourist Board

Nat. Tourismus Organisation Serbiens,/Milan Simic

Iron Gate Natural Park

The Porţile de Fier (Iron Gate) Natural Park, located on the Romanian bank, extends over 1,156 sq km (446 sq miles) from the river Nera to the west to the Đerdap 1 to the east. Its breathtaking landscapes and seascapes are protected by the International Union for the Conservation of Nature (IUCN).

Kazan Narrows

With the Kazan Narrows (km 974–965) you come to the most spectacular stretch of gorges. Ships are obliged to pass singly through the entrance and exit of the **Great Kazan** or Cazanele Mari (km 974–970), because the navigable channel is scarcely 100 m wide, with a strong current and riverbed over 80 m deep.

At **Dubova** (km 970), the Danube widens into a bay only to then immediately revert to the picturesque narrows of the **Small Kazan** or Cazanele Mici (km 969–965), which are enhanced at km 967 on an exposed part of the Romanian bank by a small church. At the nearby mouth of the little River Mraconia, trav-

Decebalus glares at the cruise passengers passing by his image. | The Tabula Trajana, Roman history on the Danube. | In the distance the river narrows at the Iron Gate.

ellers are watched over by the grim face of **Decebalus**, last prince of the Dracians (87–106), a 40-m relief sculpted in the rock.

Tabula Trajana

On the right bank, look out for the weathered marble Trajan's Plaque (km 965) set here in AD 101 in honour of the Roman emperor. In a few unpretentious words, it commemorates the construction of Trajan's Road along the Danube, a great feat for the time. The plaque was actually moved a little further up the bank from its original position when the reservoir was built.

Orşova

The riverbed widens into the Orşova Basin (km 965–950). Excursion ships dock at the Serbian town of Tekija (km 956). Opposite, the railway and busy European motorway E70 lead down to the deeply indented Bay of Orşova (km 954). The village lies in the greenery on the west side of the bay, crowned by the **St Ana convent**, while the view on the east side is dictated by the activity of the modern harbour and its wharves. Unfortunately nothing could be done to save the old town of Orşova, which dated back to the Roman settlement of Tierna, the end point of Trajan's Road; it disappeared beneath the waters when the river was dammed.

Băile Herculane

From Orşova you can make an interesting side-trip to the nearby spa of Băile Herculane (Baths of Hercules) in the narrow Cerna valley, 17 km north of the river. These hot sulphurous springs (over 40 °C) set amidst delightful countryside have lost none of the popularity they used to enjoy in Roman times. In the 19th century the spa resort was frequented by a wealthy clientèle mainly made up of members of the Austro-Hungarian bourgeoisie. Franz-Joseph and his wife each had their own pavilion. People came to cure rheumatism, as well as nervous and digestive problems. In winter, you can ski on nearby slopes.

Iron Gate:
Đerdap Power Station

The Iron Gate was opened to large ships after the inauguration of the gigantic Đerdap hydroelectric power station in 1971, a joint venture between Romania and Serbia. To pass the Iron Gate in the old days, your ship would have been towed by locomotive and tug along a canal to avoid the danger spot. The riverscape has greatly changed, but at least ships can now sail cheerfully through.

At the **Đerdap 1** Locks (km 943), it takes 90 minutes for boats to clear the 34-m lift in the step-locks' two boat tanks, each 310 m long and 30 m wide.

The mighty Belogradchik Fortress, known as Kaleto, is one of the best-preserved strongholds in Bulgaria.

Ada Kaleh

The island of Ada Kaleh (km 952) suffered the same fate as ancient Orşova and Trajan's Road when the dam was built for the hydro-electric plant at the Iron Gate. A fragment of the Orient in the middle of the Danubian region was lost, its Turkish coffee houses, picturesque alleys and gardens, and its characteristic atmosphere submerged for ever beneath the river. Attempts were made to rescue a few buildings on **Şimian Island** further downstream (km 927).

Drobeta-Turnu Severin

The ancient Dacian settlement of Drobeta-Turnu Severin (km 931) takes you far back from the achievements of the 20th century. Under orders from Emperor Trajan, the architect Apollodorus of Damascus built a bridge across the Danube here in AD 103. With 20 arches, it was one of the longest in the empire. The bridge was demolished under Hadrian, Trajan's successor, but two of its piers have survived to the present day, and testify to the high level of sophistication the Dacian civilization had attained, such as villages with timber houses and linen clothing with Thracian-style trousers.

The **Iron Gates Museum** (Muzeul Regiunii Porților De Fier) at 2, Strada Independenței, provides a fascinating glimpse of the region's natural and cultural history. The **Art Museum** or Muzeul de Artă, located in a monumental building with Baroque stucco decorations at 3, Str. Rahovei, displays works by Romanian artists.

Đerdap 2

The widening Danube emerges from the mountains in broad loops and arrives after 80 km at Đerdap 2 (km 863), where at the second of Serbia's and Romania's jointly operated power stations the locks have a hoist of only 10 m to clear.

Walachia

The mouth of the **River Timok** (km 846) marks the border between Serbia and Bulgaria. The Danube enters the great plain of Walachia, flowing wide and powerful and forming for the next 470 km (290 miles) the frontier between Romania and Bulgaria. Each uses its own version of the name: on the Romanian bank the Dunărea flows past flat lands studded with reed-fringed lakes, whilst the Bulgarian bank of the Dunav is often steep and rocky. As the river used to burst its banks here frequently in former times, noone risked building villages by the water's edge.

New Europe Bridge

In 2013, the New Europe Bridge (also called Calafat-Vidin Bridge) linked Calafat (km 796) to the harbour town of Vidin. **Calafat**, once a fortified city founded by Genoese colonists and now an industrial centre, played a key part in the Crimean War in the 19th century.

Vidin

Vidin (km 790) is one of the most ancient towns in Bulgaria. Both Celts and Thracians valued this favourable location on the Danube, and the Romans built the fortress of Bononia here, destroyed several times by the Huns and Avars. The town's heyday was in the 14th century when, under the name of Bdin, it was capital of the principality of the same name, but it fell to the Ottomans in 1396. The Turkish feudal lord Osman Pazvantoğlu took it as his own personal fief from 1793 to 1807.

The Orthodox **Cathedral of St Dimitar**, the second largest in Bulgaria, has icons and frescoes. Be sure also to see the mausoleum-like **library** (ca. 1800) of Osman Pazvantoğlu, who had rebelled against the Sultan.

The **mosque** is built in typical oriental style but instead of the crescent moon that normally tops the dome, here it is an arrowhead—eloquent testimony to its builder's insubordination. The ruins of the old **synagogue** can still be seen.

The fortress of **Baba Vida**, on the river bank in the north part of the park, dates back to the 10th century and was extended and strengthened in the 14th century. Today it serves as backdrop for theatrical performances.

Belogradchik

From Vidin in the Danube plain, an excursion of just 50 km (around 30 miles) goes into the wooded foothills of the Balkans to the little hill town of Belogradchik nestling against a grandiose backdrop of russet-hued rocks. Winds and rains have carved the

SOFIA

The long 4-hour approach to Sofia from Nikopol or Vidin adds to the excursion to the Bulgarian capital with its passage through widely varying landscapes from the Danube plain into the dramatic Balkan mountains.

Sofia sits in a broad valley at an altitude of 550 m between the emblematic **Vitosha** mountain range to the south and the **Stara Planina** (Balkan Mountains) to the north. The Bulgarians affirm that it is one of Europe's most ancient cities, founded 5,000 years ago. When Bulgarian members of parliament chose it as their national capital in 1879, it numbered only 12,000 inhabitants. Viennese architects came to the aid of the Bulgarians to turn it into a real city. The city has retained something of the Mitteleuropa of its beginnings, with its royal palace, buildings from the 1900s and its numerous parks.

The **presidential offices** are guarded by two soldiers in ceremonial white uniform with scarlet collar and an ostrich-feathered *kalpak* fur hat. The grand changing of the guard takes place at 10 a.m. with simpler versions performed every hour. Beyond the main entrance you can see in the middle of the great courtyard Sofia's most ancient edifice, the **St George Rotunda**, a round red-brick church original built at the end of the Roman Empire, probably in the 4th century.

The heart of the ancient and medieval city came close to **Maria Luiza Boulevard**, which thronged with traffic leads to the Vladaïska river, spammed by the pretty **Lions' Bridge**. On the

hemis.fr/Perousse

Watchful soldiers are on guard outside the presidential offices.

way, you will see the 16th-century **Banya Bashi Mosque** or Mosque of Baths, still active.

Tsar Osvoboditel Boulevard, main thoroughfare of the town's historic centre, runs straight west-east between the **TZUM** Central Department Store (the name of a former communist shop) and the University.

The **Archaeological Museum** is housed in the Great Mosque (*Büyük camii*) built by the Turks in the late 15th century. Its collections trace the history of the country from its origins to the Middle Ages. The finest pieces are on the ground floor, devoted to classical antiquity and the Early Christian era. The most renowned exhibit is the Thracian treasure of Valchitran, comprising 13 pieces in 12.5 kg of pure gold.

A vast esplanade with shady gardens, **Alexander Battenberg Square** southeast of the St George Retunda is the true heart of the city. **Ivan Vazov National Theatre,** built in 1907, dominates the square with its neoclassical pediment.

The fine creamy yellow façade of the neo-baroque Royal Palace opens out onto the esplanade. It was built in 1889 as a home for Prince Alexander Battenberg after his election. Today, it houses the **National Art Gallery,** exhibiting collections of Bulgarian art from the Middle Ages to the present day, and the **National Ethnographic Museum,** displaying jewellery, costumes, embroidery, carpets and furniture.

The vast **Alexander Nevsky Square**, with its cathedral towering above it in the centre, is where Sofia was reborn at the end of the 19th century. All the great national buildings rise up around it: the National Assembly, Academy of Sciences, National Library and the University. The **Cathedral** is dedicated to Alexander Nevsky, the patron saint of Russia's Orthodox church. The monumental sanctuary is crowned with gilded cupolas. Some 200 icons are displayed in the crypt. The eternal flame of the monument to the Unknown Soldier faces the Cathedral and points the way to the **St Sophia Church**. This austere 6th century brick edifice is one of the oldest in Sofia.

Vitosha Boulevard, a bustling shopping street, is lined with several fashionable boutiques and extends towards the monumental Communist-era **Palace of Culture**.

The neighbourhood of Boyana, beyond the city's peripheral ring road, is famous for its medieval church. Indeed, the **Boyana Church** has been declared a UNESCO World Heritage Site for the exceptional quality of its frescoes.

conglomerate of sandstone into bizarre gigantic pillars. To control the Balkan passage, the Romans built a guard-post in the 1st century as an eyrie up in a striking ensemble of towering rocks, a wildly romantic fort which Turks and Bulgars subsequently took over.

Lom

Lom (km 743) is Bulgaria's second-largest Danube port, after Ruse. It was built on the site of a Roman fortification, **Almus**, which is still partially visible in the residential area of Kaletata. Finds from Roman times can be seen in the town's **Museum of History**, housed in the old town hall at 6, Eremia Bulgarski Street.

The city also has a 500-m long pebble beach at the bank of the Danube.

Kozloduy

The next Bulgarian town of importance is Kozloduy (km 700), with its nuclear power station. The town was the site of a dramatic incident in 1876. Bulgarian poet and freedom fighter Christo Botev forced the captain of the Danube steamer *Radetzky* to moor here, so that he and his followers could take up the fight against the Turks. He and his comrades-in-arms lost their lives, but to this day their act of bravery is commemorated by flowers laid on the river bank. The Radetzky ship-museum has a 1966 replica of the steamship moored to the pier.

Oryahovo

High up in a picturesque landscape of cornfields and vineyards, the town of Oryahovo (km 678) is an agricultural centre.

Gigen

Near to the small port of **Baykal** at the mouth of the **Iskar** (km 636), important finds from Roman times were unearthed at Gigen. The foundations of a large temple, precious mosaics, paved streets, water mains and sewers indicate that this was the site of the Roman town of **Ulpia Oescus**. A 10th-century inscription in Old Bulgarian was discovered in the old **Church of St George**. On the Romanian bank, you pass by **Corabia** (km 630), a centre for sugar refinery. Mineral oil is trans-shipped in the Bulgarian town of **Somovit** (km 608).

Nikopol

Nikopol (km 597) also looks back to a Roman past. Trajan achieved a major victory over the Dacians here and named the fort "Town of the Victory on the Lower Danube"

(Nicopolis ad Istrum). In 629 the Byzantine Emperor Heraclius had the fortress extended. The Turks strengthened it further, but in 1877 the Russians pulled down the massive fortifications. The ruins are still worth a visit, and you might also like to peep into the small 13th-century church nearby.

Turnu Măgurele

Opposite Nikopol and linked by ferry is the port and fertilizer factory of Turnu Măgurele, with its population of about 30,000.

Pleven

From Nikopol you can take an overland trip to Pleven, the biggest and most important town on the Danube plain. It was settled in prehistoric times (4th to 3rd millennium BC), and then variously held, much later, by the Thracians,

Romans, Slavs and Turks. Pleven's centre may surprise you with its well-kept bourgeois buildings, fountains and artificial waterfalls in the pedestrian zone. Several churches are worth a visit, as are the **Regional Historical Museum** (3, Stoyan Zaimov) and the nearby **Mausoleum**, which commemorates the Russian and Romanian troops who fell in 1877. The historic battle for Pleven is depicted in the circular **Pleven Panorama** set in Skobelev Park.

Belene Island
Between km 577 and km 560, you pass by the Bulgarian island of Belene (Ostrov Persin), whose once infamous concentration camp for political prisoners is not visible from the river. The island is part of the **Persina Nature Park**, which stretches over 217 sq km (84 sq miles) and contains two island groups.

Svishtov
At Svishtov (km 554), the Danube approaches its southernmost point. The terraced layout of the town on the hilly banks above the river gives it a particular charm. Among the sights in this major port are two unusual 17th-century underground churches, as well as the **Holy Trinity Church** and the **Aleko Konstantinov House-Museum** dedicated to the famous Bulgarian writer, shot dead in 1897.

Veliko Tarnovo
Excursions also go to picturesque Veliko Tarnovo, medieval capital of Bulgaria (1187–1396), also known as the City of the Tsars. It is almost encircled by the **Yantra river**, the houses clinging to the steep sides of the gorge.

Tsarevets Hill
Watching over it all, the **Tsarevets Fortress** stands on a spectacular peninsula enclosed by a meander of the river. Easy to defend, the site was occupied by the Thracians, then by all the other tribes that ruled Bulgaria. In the 12th century, two boyar brothers, Asen and Peter, declared the end of Byzantine rule in Bulgaria and proclaimed the city a capital. A period of great prosperity began.

Trapezitsa Hill
In the Middle Ages, the nobles settled on the hill facing the fortress, while the merchants and craftsmen resided in the lower town. Tarnovo soon became one of the main political and cultural centres of eastern Europe, renowned for its art school. The Turks took the city in 1393, putting an end to its golden age, but its medieval atmosphere remains. The shops along the cobbled streets around **Samovodska Charshia** are a delight.

Apart from the lovely old houses, there are several churches and museums well worth exploring. Among these are the **Archaeological Museum**, the **Museum of the Bulgarian Revival and the Constituent Assembly** and the **Sarafkina House Museum**.

Arbanassi

The village of Arbanassi, also transliterated as Arbanasi, lies some 10 minutes' drive away from Veliko Tarnovo, and it is worth a visit for the originality of its fortified houses and the beauty of the frescoes in the **Nativity Church**, the best-known of the five churches built in the 16th and 17th centuries.

The 17th century **Konstantsalieva House**, once belonging to a rich merchant, was later restored in National Revival style and converted into an attractive ethnographic museum.

Ruse

Ruse (km 495), with about 157,000 inhabitants, is Bulgaria's biggest Danube port. Back when the Roman fleet was stationed here, the place was called Sextanta Prista ("Sixty Ships"). A new settlement under the name of Ruse (or Rousse) is first men-

www.velikoturnovo.info

Claude Hervé-Bazin

Nat. Tourismus Organisation Serbiens

The splendid Nativity Church in Arbanassi. | Roses are one of Bulgaria's main exports. | Veliko Tarnovo's Patriarchal church and Tsarevets Fortress.

tioned at the beginning of the 16th century; the Turks later named it Ruschuk. In the 19th century the first railway in the Ottoman Empire (from Ruschuk to Varna on the Black Sea) was opened here. In the **Rousse Regional Historical Museum** you can find out more about the history of the city and the surrounding region.

Little of historical interest has survived, although the neo-baroque buildings in the city centre give Ruse the appearance of an old Austrian provincial town. Sights include the **Holy Trinity Church** (Sveta Troitsa) of 1764 with its beautiful icons and frescoes and the imposing **Dohodno Zdanie** (1902), one of the symbols of the city. The seven stone sculptures on the roof personify art, science, agriculture, crafts, trade, defense and the free flight of

spirit. The old railway station, built in 1866 and situated on the banks of the Danube, was the first in the country. Today it houses the **National Transport Museum**, which displays steam engines and railroad carriages. Opposite the Hotel Riga, the **Urban Lifestyle of Ruse Museum** occupies the handsome wooden Kaliopa House.

For rest and recreation, the inhabitants of this industrial town have many parks to choose from, as well as the **Lipnik Forest Park** 12 km (7.5 miles) away.

Ivanovo

Another worthwhile excursion is to the cliff monasteries of Ivanovo (12th–15th centuries) with their unique murals, listed by UNESCO. The most exceptional are the ones in the **Church of the Virgin Mary**, representing biblical scenes.

Giurgiu

Prior to the construction of the bridge at Vindin, the only Danube bridge between Romania and Bulgaria was the 2224-m Friendship Bridge (km 489) built in 1954. These days it's simply called **Danube Bridge**. Trains travel over the steel structure into the Romanian town of Giurgiu (km 493) on the lower level and cars on the upper level. The name originates from Genoese sailors who built a trading station and a castle, San Giorgio, here in the 14th century. Of the Turkish fortress only a watchtower in the town centre remains. The Orient Express, the long-distance passenger rail which operated from 1883 to 2009, ran from Paris to Giurgiu, where passengers were ferried across the Danube to Ruse to pick up another train to Varna on the Black Sea.

Bucharest

Most people landing in Giurgiu do not stay in town but head for Bucharest, 64 km away. Bucharest is the political, economical and cultural centre of the country, in the heart of Walachia. The city spreads along the banks of the Dâmboviţa, a tributary of the Danube, and the first written documents mentioning the city were signed by Prince Vlad Ţepeş, "the Impaler", ruler of Walachia and model for Dracula, on September 20, 1459. Over the centuries the city endured several dark periods and catastrophic events, notably its destruction by the Turks in 1595. In 1659, it became capital of Walachia and then, two centuries later (1862), of the principality formed by the reunion of Walachia and Moldavia. It was designated capital of

Sandu Mandrea

Claude Hervé-Bazin

the Kingdom of Romania in 1881. During its golden age, between the two world wars, the city was redesigned by French and Romanian architects trained in Paris. The streets were transformed into tree-lined boulevards and a triumphal arch was erected, earning Bucharest the title of "Little Paris of the East". Romania became a NATO member in 2004 and joined the EU in 2007. Of its some 20 million inhabitants, 2 million live in Bucharest, most of them in the wide belt of apartment buildings encircling the city centre. The majority (around 90%) are Orthodox.

Piaţa Unirii

Start your sightseeing in Old Bucharest at Piaţa Unirii. The square is about two-thirds of the way along Bulevardul Unirii, the long avenue studded by 41 fountains, each representing the country's 41 districts, culminating in Ceauşescu's huge palace. Look along the esplanade covering the river, lined with boutiques and shopping centres. This was the former Avenue of the Victory of Socialism, 100 m wide, which the citizens referred to as Kitsch Boulevard during Ceauşescu's rule.

The old Caru' cu Bere is famous for its traditional plates and authentic Romanian environment. | Picturesque frescoes in the Stavropoleos church.

Parliament Palace

At the far western end of Bulevardul Unirii is the enormous Parliament Palace (Palatul Parlamentului), the house that Ceauşescu built. Perched on top of an artificial hill riddled with secret passages and anti-atomic shelters, it is something of a national embarrassment. A fantasy of marble and gilt, it has 1,100 rooms (second in size only to the Pentagon), secret passageways and nuclear shelters. To clear away the area for its construction, 40,000 inhabitants were displaced and a fifth of the old town was destroyed, including 19 churches, 9 of which were listed historic monuments. Inside, the floors are marble, the walls lined with walnut and cherry panelling, the ceilings six storeys high. The infamous Ceauşescu couple never had time to enjoy their palace; it was still unfinished when they were executed in 1989. At present it is the seat of parliament and a congress centre in addition to housing the **National Contemporary Art Museum**, dedicated mainly to Romanian artists.

Curtea Veche

Near Piaţa Unirii stand the remains of Curtea Veche (Old Courtyard), the palace of Vlad Ţepeş, residence of the princes of Walachia and the only vestige of the medieval city. It was built in the 15th century and expanded by Constantin Brancovan (1688–1714). Destroyed by fire and earthquake, it was abandoned in the 18th century. Little remains of the original vaulted halls and the luxuriant gardens.

The **Church of Curtea Veche** (Biserica Curtea Veche), at the corner of Strada Franceză and Strada Şepcari, was founded in the middle of the 16th century during the reign of Prince Mircea Ciobanu. The Walachian princes were sworn in here. Opposite the church, **Hanul lui Manuc** is a historical inn built round a central courtyard by an Armenian merchant in 1808. It is worth a visit for its characteristic architecture.

The Old Trading District

The most important sights of Bucharest are north of the Dâmboviţa, particularly in the area bound by Calea Victoriei and the parallel Bulevardul Magheru, which changes its name to Bulevardul Bălcescu as it progresses.

In the 16th and 17th centuries the **Lipscani Quarter** was the city's economic and political centre; the name came from the city of Leipzig, as many goods were imported from there. Its southern boundary is the Dâmboviţa, in the west Calea Victoriei and in the north boulevards Regina Elisabeta and Carol I, while in the east it stops at Bulevardul Brătianu. Many shops have appeared among the old baroque buildings, making a lively atmosphere. One can also stroll around the **Pasajul Latin**, an underground passageway decorated with bas-reliefs that passes under the boulevard.

Around Stavropoleos Church

Bucharest is graced by numerous churches; perhaps the most attractive is located just north of Piaţa Unirii. On the street of the same name, **Stavropoleos Church** was built in 1724 when Bucharest was governed by a Phanariot from Constantinople. Oriental influence is evident in the arabesques and arcades; the frescoes are painted in the icon style, with gold leaf. In the same street, opposite the church, stands the old brasserie **Caru' cu Bere** (literally, Beer Wagon), worth visiting for its exuberant décor of painted woodwork, arched vaulting, frescoes and stained-glass windows. A short walk away, at the crossroads with Calea Victoriei, stands a pompous building that houses the **National History Museum** (Muzeul Naţional de Istorie a României). It was originally the post office, built in neoclassical style in 1900. Among the many thousands of exhibits, the most interesting are the Daco-Roman collections and the Treasury. Opposite the museum stands the **CEC Palace** (Palatul C.E.C), now the headquarters of the CEC Bank.

Close by, **Pasajul Macca-Vila-crosse**, a glass-roofed shopping arcade, stretches between Victoriei and Carada streets. To the northeast, in Strada Ion Ghica, is the Russian-Orthodox **Biserica Rusă** (or St Nicholas Church) with its onion domes (1905–09). At the intersection of Brătianu Avenue and Ion Ghica, the little Şuţu Palace, a handsome neo-Gothic building enhanced by a wrought-iron and glass porch, was built from 1833 to 1835 for a Marshal of the court. It now houses the **Municipal Museum** (Muzeul municipiului), tracing the development of the capital in photographs and other displays.

From Piaţa Universitaţii to the North

Piaţa Universitatii is one of the busiest squares of the city, dominated by the tower of the Inter-Continental Hotel and the modern **Ion Luca Caragiale National Theatre** (Teatrul Naţional I. L. Caragiale). West of the square is the Second-Empire style university building.

Walking up Calea Victoriei you will see, on the left, the red-brick Creţúlescu Church, topped by two domes. Immediately behind it, on Revolution Square, is the imposing neoclassical building of the **National Museum of Art of Romania** (Muzeul Naţional de Artă al României) on the corner of Strada Ştirbei Vodă. This building was the Palace of the Republic, damaged during the December Revolution, when the collections were severely depleted. Paintings by Romanian and European artists are displayed, in addition to works from the Far East. Opposite stands the **Central University Library** with its neoclassical columns. North of it, just across Benjamin Franklin street, the imposing **Ateneul Român**, beneath a great dome, was built between 1886 and 1888 by a French architect.

At the northern end of Calea Victoriei is the eclectic Cantacuzino Palace (1898) housing the **George Enescu Museum** (Muzeul Naţional George Enescu).

To Herăstrău Park

The majestic Şoseaua Kiseleff Boulevard, shaded by tall trees, leads north from Victoriei Square to the Triumphal Arch and Herăstrău Park. Along the way, don't miss the **Museum of the Romanian Peasant**, displaying traditional costumes, icons and cooking utensils from another era. The **Arcul de Triumf**, on the square of the same name, is similar to the one in Paris, but only half the size. It was first built of wood in 1922, then in stone in 1935, to the memory of World War I soldiers.

Frédérique Fasser

Claude Hervé-Bazin

An old window preserved in the Village Museum. | **The Palace of Parliament is one of the world's largest buildings.**

Danube Writers. Panait Istrati (1884–1935) was the son of a Greek smuggler in Brăila. He led an adventurous life and celebrated the magic of the Bărăgan steppes and the banks of the Danube writing mostly in French, a language which he had taught himself. **Elias Canetti** (1905–94) describes his birthplace, Ruse, which at that time still went by its Turkish name, in his autobiography: "Ruschuk [...] was a marvellous town [...], inhabited by people of the most varied origins; on any one day you could hear seven or eight languages spoken." In his childhood, the main languages were Spanish, his mother tongue, and Bulgarian; he used German to write his books, for which he was awarded the Nobel Prize in 1981.

Herăstrău Park, north of the Triumphal Arch, contains the fascinating **Village Museum** (Muzeul Satului). Founded in 1936 by Dimitrie Gusti, a professor of sociology, it assembles 300 wooden buildings brought here from the four corners of Romania.

Cotroceni Palace

On Bulevardul Geniului to the west of the city centre, in a magnificent setting of wooded gardens, the Cotroceni Palace was built in 1893 for Princess Marie. In addition to being residence of the President of the Republic, it is also used for concerts and houses a museum displaying interesting medieval collections.

Behind the palace, the **Botanical Garden** (Grădina Botanică) was created in 1884–85 and covers 17 ha planted with many species.

Olteniţa

The industrial and warehouse town of Olteniţa (km 430) is a common starting point for tourists heading to or coming from Bucharest. The **Muzeul Civilizaţiei Gumelniţa** displays finds from the Neolithic settlement revealed on Gumelniţa hill near the city.

Tutrakan

Opposite, the Bulgarian town of Tutrakan is an important fisheries centre and was already a stronghold back in Roman times. It is a good starting point for outings in the hinterland.

Srebarna Nature Reserve

Bird-spotters take up positions on the heights of the island of Vetren (km 358), **Ostrovul Ciocăneşti**, to look out for rare species heading for the 6-sq-km reserve around Lake Srebarna. The reserve was established in 1942 and is inscribed on the UNESCO World Heritage List. Among the breeders are the curly-feathered Dalmatian pelicans and six varieties of heron, including the purple and squacco herons. Various kites and falcons can be seen circling overhead and numerous species of duck nest or spend the winter in the reserve.

Silistra

Silistra (km 376), close to the Bulgarian-Romanian border, was founded by Trajan in the 2nd century. In 1942 a Roman tomb was discovered here with very beautiful, well-preserved mural paintings from the 4th century, depicting scenes of family life, hunting, plants and birds. The old Turkish fortress of Silistra has also resisted the ravages of time.

Negotiating the narrow waterways of the Danube Delta.

To the Delta

From km 374 the Danube flows entirely through Romanian territory for the next 240 km. Before emptying itself into the Black Sea, the river divides into several branches.

Dobrogea and Bărăgan

On the right bank begins the Dobrogea plateau, stretching all the way to the Black Sea; the Bărăgan plain on the left bank is reminiscent of the Hungarian puszta. The bygone romanticism of this steppe landscape has been captured in the books of the Romanian writer Panait Istrati.

Borcea Branch

At km 371, the Danube divides into two arms, the Borcea Branch (Brațul Borcea) and the main river, coming together again at km 248 to embrace the Balta Ialomiței island area. The 100-km Brațul Borcea is deeper and 23 km shorter than the main river, with both routes serving ship traffic. From **Călărași** (km 97 of the Brațul Borcea) a ferry sails to the Bulgarian town of Silistra and a Romanian ferry serves **Ostrov** (km 367).

From Ostrov, the road snakes through a beautiful area to **Adamclisi**, where a Roman memorial, the **Tropaeum Traiani**, commemorates Trajan's decisive victory over the Dacians.

Excursion to Constanța

From Adamclisi, the road continues through the vineyards of Murfatlar, which produce a sweet white dessert wine of the same name, to reach Constanța, Romania's biggest seaport.

Constanța is also the terminus of the 64-km (40-mile) **Danube-Black Sea Canal**, completed in 1983, which starts in Cernavodă. (The canal divides again, with a northern arm leading to Năvodari.)

Cernavodă

In Cernavodă (km 300), which means "Black Water", the Danube is at its closest to the Black Sea. Another great feat of engineering is the railway bridge built in 1895, which over a distance of 15 km crosses the Danube, Ialomița Island and the Brațul Borcea as far as Fetești (km 36 of the Brațul Borcea). It was a significant aid in the economic development of the Danubian region. Today, Cernavodă and Fetești are also linked by motorway.

Ghindărești

After Cernavodă the river turns northwards. On the right bank, Ghindărești (km 260) comes into view, a small, old Russian fishing village in a very picturesque location. The domes of the **Orthodox Church** have a silvery gleam.

Hârşova

Like most places on the lower Danube, Hârşova (km 253) was a Roman camp and later a Turkish fortress. The fine Russian Orthodox church was founded by the Lipovan religious group, which is now mainly to be found in the delta. After the **Ialomiţa River** flows into the Borcea Branch, the latter joins up again with the main river. The Danube Valley narrows for a few kilometres. Today, a road bridge heading for **Giurgeni** on the left bank crosses the river at km 238; in earlier times, shepherds from Transylvania used to cross here to graze their flocks on the fertile Dobrogea plain.

Brăila

After the narrows, the river divides up again and forms a 60-km-long landscape of islands and beds of reeds, the **Balta Mică a Brăilei Natural Park**, reuniting with the Danube at Brăila itself (km 170). This port, which was first mentioned in 1368, was fought over fiercely in the Middle Ages. For 300 years it was defended by a Turkish fortress, finally pulled down in 1829. Today Brăila is home to various industries; the reeds from the Danube delta are processed here. Brăila is the birthplace of the Romanian writer Panait Istrati. He published in French; his best-known work is *The Confession of a Loser*.

Galaţi

The town of Galaţi (km 150) was founded 500 years ago but it doesn't look its age, for heavy damage in World War II left nothing of the old centre. As in Brăila, all life centres round the harbour, which has a large shipyard.

Between the mouths of the two large tributaries **Siret** and **Prut**, the Danube makes its last decisive turn to the east. Along the lower reaches of the Prut runs the border between Romania and Moldova, formed as an independent republic in 1991. From its mouth at km 134 for about half a kilometre, the two countries share a common Danube border, therefore at km 133, the left bank is already part of Ukraine, and for the next 53 km, the Danube forms the Ukrainian-Romanian border.

Reni

The next sizeable town, Reni (km 128), is an important Ukrainian commercial port. On the right bank you will pass by the former Turkish fortress of **Isaccea** (km 103). Its name derives from the Turkish Isak-Kioi ("Isaac's Village").

Honey is harvested from bees that feed in the extensive linden woodlands of the region; tobacco cultivation, wine-making and fishing are other important sources of income.

The Danube Delta

The Danube delta is a world apart. To this day, barely a road crosses this watery kingdom, and the only way to explore the streams, the waterlily-carpeted lakes and the lonely fishing villages is by boat. In the delta the Danube splits into three main arms: to the north the Chilia, which for almost its entire length forms the border between Ukraine and Romania, in the middle the canalized Sulina branch, the main thoroughfare for shipping traffic, and in the south the Sfântu Gheorghe branch, the oldest and most unspoilt.

Danube Delta Biosphere Reserve

The vast delta is shared between Romania, which owns four-fifths of the area, and Ukraine. With the immense lagoons of Razim and Sinoie, it covers more than 6000 sq km (over 1900 sq miles), of which half are protected by UNESCO as a Biosphere Reserve. The silt carried by the current has created a labyrinth of channels, nearly 400 lakes, spongy islands *(plauri)*, meadows and dunes linked by a vast network of canals. In some places you'll see

This part of the world has hardly changed in 100 years. | Two members of the delta bird-world: a family of pelicans and a grey heron. Don't forget your binoculars.

istockphoto.com/F. Kienas

Romanian Tourist Office

Romanian Tourist Office

Animal Kingdom. Tulcea and Vylkove are the usual starting points for excursions into the delta to see its flora and fauna, unique in Europe.

In the marshes, there are eight different members of the heron family alone, including grey, purple and great white herons, little egrets and bitterns, as well as Dalmatian and white pelicans, storks, ibises, spoonbills and white-tailed eagles. Cormorants perch on the bank, drying their wings.

The land-based fauna include wildcats, wolves, wild boar, foxes and otters. The waters teem with fish, which form the staple diet of the human and animal inhabitants: pike, carp, pike-perch, catfish, tench, perch and bream, and sturgeon regularly swim up from the Black Sea. But freshwater herring are the fisherman's most important catch.

Romanian Tourist Office

elevated grinds, plateaux formed by deposits where trees have taken root. Reeds are everywhere and serve a useful purpose: they filter the polluted waters coming from upstream. A transition between the earth, the river and the sea, the immense delta, at the confluence of five migratory routes, is also the refuge of some 300 species of birds.

The Inhabitants of the Delta

Here and there, you will see tiny villages of reed-thatched houses, blending in perfectly with their surroundings and accessible only by boat. For several days each spring, the river floods, the water seeping through the doorways and carrying away stabilized lands. The 15,000 inhabitants of the delta live mostly from collecting reeds, fish farming and traditional fishing. In majority they are Lipovans, followers of the old Orthodox rites who fled here from Russia in the 17th century in the face of persecution by the Orthodox Church; they are known as Old Believers. Their churches often hold precious icons of lime-wood (*lipa* in Russian), and their traditional costumes and customs give the visitor a vivid impression of life in old Russia. They number more than 35,000 in Romania; they cross themselves with two fingers instead of three, and the men wear long beards.

Tulcea

The largest town of the delta, with a population of 91,000, lies just before the last fork in the Danube at km 71, on the site of the ancient Roman settlement of Aegissus, built in turn on a Dacian city founded in the 7th century BC. It is a significant port and industrial centre; the harbour bustles with luxury boats taking visitors on trips into the delta.

Conceived as a museum and public aquarium, the **Eco-Tourism Centre of the Danube Delta** near the embarkment (14 Noiembrie str.) focuses on the natural patrimony of the Delta Biosphere Reserve. Just behind it is the **Art Museum** (Muzeul de Artă), displaying paintings and scuptures by prominent Romanian artists.

In the nearby **Museum of Ethnography and Folk Art**, located in the former headquarters of the National Bank of Romania, you will find agricultural and fishing tools, folk clothing and jewellery.

Chilia Branch

The northernmost branch, Chilia, is in places over 1000 m wide. Alone it carries two-thirds of the river waters to the delta. It is longer (120 km) and more tortuous than the others, and dotted with islands, and was long ignored because it marked the boundary with the Soviet Union. At its mouth, it breaks up into myriad mini-deltas.

Izmail (Ukraine)

At km 90 lies Izmail. Its fortress was built by Genoese merchants in the 12th century and from the 15th century onwards, it was the focus of fighting between the Russians and Turks. In 1790 the Russian generals Suvorov and Kutuzov succeeded in capturing the town. Suvorov is commemorated by an equestrian statue and a museum. Afterwards the town was passed back and forth between Romania, Russia and Moldova, to finally become part of independent Ukraine in 1991.

Vylkove (Ukraine)

Vylkove, the main Lipovan town (km 14), was founded in the 18th century by Cossacks. The inhabitants live from fishing and winemaking.

Sulina Branch

Downstream from Tulcea, passenger boats ply back and forth incessantly between fishing craft and rusting cargoes along the Sulina Branch. The channel was deepened back in the 19th century to permit the passage of bigger ships, and the winding 92-km stretch of river was turned into a 64-km canal with a navigable channel 150 m wide and at least 7.50 m deep. Merchandise and passengers are unloaded at regular intervals outside the little villages scattered along the banks.

www.rumaenien-tourismus.de

Sulina

Via Crişan, one of the largest fishing villages in the delta, you reach the port of Sulina, where the Danube flows into the Black Sea. You can see the **Kilometre Zero** marker near the old lighthouse. Already a settlement in Byzantine times, Sulina was later a mooring point for Genoese ships. Since the 19th-century it has developed shipyards and a fish-processing industry. Here, the work of the river is highlighted: by depositing 80 mio. tons of silt and gaining 40 m from the sea each year, it has moved the lighthouse from the shore to the middle of the marketplace!

Black Sea

From Sulina to the Black Sea, ships still have to journey another 12 km (7.5 miles) through a canal bordered by quays in order to reach the open sea. With an area of over 400,000 sq km, the Black Sea is surrounded by no less than six countries.

Sfântu Gheorghe Branch

At the mouth of the southernmost of the three arms, Sfântu Gheorghe is the headquarters of the sturgeon fishermen. The branch traces great loops until it reaches the Black Sea.

hemis.fr/Cintract

Constanţa's Cathedral. | Folk traditions are kept alive in the Dobrogea region.

CONSTANŢA

Constanţa is one of the country's principal cities and its biggest commercial sea port. When it was founded, under the name Tomis, Greek traders came to exchange their wines for Dacian grain. But the city reached its height under the Romans, when it became the main port of the Black Sea. During the reign of Augustus, the poet Ovid spent his last years here, in exile. After the fall of the Roman empire, and numerous barbarian invasions, the city sank into oblivion. Much later, around 1300, the Genoese built a harbour, and a new era of prosperity began. During the four centuries of Ottoman rule the city foundered once again, until 1878 when Dobrogea was united with Romania.

On Piaţa Ovidiu (Ovid Square), site of the agora of ancient Tomis, stands a statue of the author of the *Metamorphoses*.

The **National History and Archaeology Museum** (Muzeul de istorie naţională şi arheologie) in the old town hall displays a collection of Greco-Roman objects. A few streets to the northwest, the **Archaeological Park** (Parcul Arheologic) is strewn with vestiges of ancient buildings.

Down from Ovid Square you can see the slender minaret of the **Great Mosque** (Marea Moschee), built in 1910 on the ruins of the 1822 Mahmudia Mosque and originally known as the Carol I Mosque. If the door is open, you can climb up to get a fantastic view over the town and port. The interior is finely decorated in blue and ochre, and richly carpeted.

To the south is the Orthodox **Cathedral of Saints Peter and Paul**. It was built in the late 19th century in Greco-Roman style and holds several frescoes by Bucharest painters. To its left is the **Ion Jalea Museum of Sculpture**, dedicated to the Romanian artist who lost his left arm during World War I and created his greatest works with one hand.

On the sea front, opposite the little **aquarium**, stands the old Art Nouveau **Casino**, now abandoned. A promenade along the waterfront takes you to the 19th century **Genoese Lighthouse** (Farul Genovez) and a statue of poet Mihai Eminescu looking out to sea. Yachts and pleasure boats are anchored in the **Tomis Tourist Port**, protected by concrete dams.

Spicy Serbian fish soup cooked on an open fire, and eaten outdoors—what could be better?

DINING OUT

Your Danube cruise will take you on a culinary voyage of discovery. After the hearty dishes of Germany you enter the realm of Austrian cutlets and dumplings, cream-drenched cakes and pastries. Things spice up in Slovakia and Hungary with their homely stews, while Bulgarians sing the praises of their yoghurt, and Serbia and Romania have many tasty surprises in store.

Austria

The emperors and archdukes have gone; not so the Bohemian dumplings, Hungarian goulash, Polish stuffed cabbage and Serbian *shashlik*. But there are Austrian specialities too: *Wiener-schnitzel*, a thinly sliced cutlet of veal sauteed in a coating of egg and breadcrumbs; *Backhendl*, boned deep-fried chicken prepared like *Wienerschnitzel*; *Tafelspitz*, boiled beef, a Viennese favourite; or *Knödel*, dumplings served with soups and with the meat dish, studded with pieces of liver or bacon. Other main courses you'll find include roast meats (*Rostbraten*) with garlic, and in rural areas *Bauernschmaus*, literally "farmer's feast". With the Danube on the doorstep, fish turns up on many menus: trout, zander (pike-perch), pike and carp are prepared in various tasty ways.

Dumplings are also served as a dessert with hot apricot inside (*Marillenknödel*) or with cream cheese (*Topfenknödel*). As for

Yoghurt. The Bulgarians will not have it any other way: they insist that they invented yoghurt! According to legend, a shepherd of Stara Planina ran out of buckets to collect the milk of his ewes, and poured it into a new goatskin bag. The next morning, he discovered the milk transformed into yoghurt, thanks to a local bacteria, *Lactobacillus bulgaricus*. Some claim that yoghurt was already known to the nomadic Hunno-Bulgars who began migrating into Europe in the 2nd century. Others say that it has its origins in Central Asia, though don't try telling that to the Bulgarians, who believe it helps them live longer.

pastries, the variations of cherries, strawberries, hazelnuts, walnuts, apple and chocolate in tarts, pies, cakes and strudels are endless, and they are all even better topped with whipped cream (*mit Schlag*).

And you can join in the never-ending controversy over the famous chocolate cake, the Sachertorte — whether it should be split and sandwiched together with apricot jam, or just left plain.

The local wines are mostly white, and people are happy to drink white wine with either meat or fish. The best known, Gumpoldskirchner, has the full body and bouquet of its southern vineyards, but Grinzinger, Sieveringer and Neustifter are equally popular. From the Danube valley, with an extra natural sparkle, come the Kremser, Dürnsteiner and Langenloiser. One way to enjoy them is to visit a *Heuriger*, where you drink young white wine and help yourself to a buffet of hot and cold snacks, usually including cheese, cold meats and salads.

Bulgaria

Centuries of Turkish domination have left their mark on Bulgarian cuisine, in such dishes as *kyopolou*, a dip made from roasted and pureed aubergine (eggplant), pepper stuffed with minced meat, and kebabs (here spelt *kebap*) of beef or pork. *Banitza* is a baked cheese pastry, and *moussaka* is much like that made by Greek and Turkish neighbours. The spinach and zucchini soups are delicious, and Bulgaria claims to be the home of the world's best, most authentic and health-giving yoghurts.

The best Bulgarian wines, especially the rich reds, have made themselves an international reputation. Some of the best are made in Bordeaux style, from cabernet sauvignon and merlot grapes, but look also for the full-bodied local varietals *mavrud* and *melnik*, and the lighter *gamza*.

Croatia

The dishes you will be offered in Croatia vary greatly with the region. Along the Danube they reflect past periods of Turkish, Hungarian and Austrian influence, as in neighbouring Serbia. The cured, dried or smoked hams and salami-like sausage are excellent. You might be offered *burek*, a meat pie made from beef and onions, stews of sausage and beans, and for dessert, *Bregovska pita*, a delicious version of Viennese apple strudel.

Very drinkable red and white wines come from the Croatia's Dalmatian coast and offshore islands, and the locals regard no occasion as complete without a shot or two of *šljivovica*, plum brandy.

Germany

Traditional German food relies heavily on soups, stews, roasts and many varieties of sausage. The Danube flows through Bavaria, known for its beer and for its *Weisswürste*, white veal sausages flavoured with pepper and onions and served with sweet mustard. The locals like to eat them as a midday snack before starting on a proper lunch. Try also *Blaue Zipfel*, finger-sized sausages poached with onions in vinegar, and grilled *Bratwürste*. A favourite soup is *Leberknödelsuppe*, liver dumplings in beef bouillon. Main dishes include *Kalbsvögerl*, veal roll stuffed with onion, morel mushrooms, garlic and sour cream, and *Schweinebraten*, roast pork with herbs.

Succumb to desserts such as *Schmarren*, baked pancakes with apples and raisins, and *Zwetschgendatschi*, pastry with plums, cinnamon and sugar.

Germany's wines, predominantly white, are many and varied and to foreigners may seem confusingly named. But among them there is something to suit most tastes, whether as an apéritif or to go with dinner. Franconia, the

istockphoto.com/izso

Österreich Werbung

Serbian National Tourist Board

Touristinenformation Linz

A varied menu: Hungarian goulasch; Viennese schnitzel; excellent wines from Serbia; jam-filled, trellised Linzertorte.

region around Würzburg and Bamberg, produces fresh white wines to put in its famous bock-beutel, round-bellied bottles.

Hungary

A popular appetizer is *libamáj-pástétom*, flaky pastry filled with goose-liver pâté. *Hortobágyi húsos palacsinta* are pancakes filled with minced meat and sour cream; *gombafejek rántva*, bread-crumb-coated fried mushrooms. Now for the goulash, which is not at all a spicy stew, but a thinnish soup. Called *gulyásleves*, it combines bits of beef, vegetables, caraway seeds and paprika for colour and zing. *Szegedi halászlé* is a freshwater fish soup.

For the fish course, try *paprikás ponty*, carp with paprika sauce; *rácponty*, carp stew with sour cream; or *pisztráng tejszín mártásbán*, baked trout with cream.

Hungarians are extremely fond of large helpings of meat. *Pörkölt* or *bográcsgulyás* is the spicy stew that non-Hungarians call goulash. On menus you'll see *paprikás csirke*, chicken with sour cream and paprika. *Töltött paprika* are stuffed peppers; *bélszín Budapest módra* is a thick beef steak served with a sauce of peppers, mushrooms, peas and chopped chicken livers.

The Hungarians excel in the dessert department, so be sure to save room for a strudel *(rétes)* filled with *almás* (apple), *mákos* (poppy seeds), *meggyes* (sour cherries) or *túrós* (lemon, raisins and cottage cheese); or *Gundel palacsinta*, pancakes with a rich filling of chopped walnuts and raisins, covered in chocolate sauce and flambéed with brandy or rum.

Romania

Romanian cuisine can be fairly described as hearty. Staples are potatoes and a corn mash similar to Italian polenta *(mamaliga)*, while the star of the meat department is pork, usually in the form of chops or sausages. Food tends to be bland rather than spicy, and vegetarians will not have an easy time.

Lunch often consists of soup: *bortsch*, made from beetroot and giblets; sour-tasting *ciorba*, based on fermented bran, with various additions such as tripe, potatoes, marrow-bones or chicken; *colesa*, made from boletus mushrooms.

At dinner, a large dish of cold meats, liver pâté and salami is often served as hors-d'œuvre. The main course may be tasty *sarmalés*, cabbage leaves stuffed with minced beef and rice, braised until golden and served with *mamaliga*; then comes another hearty course of roast chicken *(pui)* with fried potatoes and a sauce of crushed garlic, vinegar and water, or grilled cutlets *(muschiu)* of pork *(porc)* or beef *(vaca)*, with tiny spicy pork sausages *(mititei)*.

Vegetables, served separately, are usually slices of aubergine or peppers braised in oil, or fat gherkins. Salads *(salata)* are rarely more varied than lettuce, tomato and cucumber.

Cheese is either yellow and compact *(cascaval)* or white and crumbly *(urda* or *brinza)*. Dessert may be fruit, ice cream, or, on special occasions, an elaborate gâteau with several layers of cream and frosted topping.

Meals might begin (and end) with a small glass of *tsuica*, a heady plum brandy to be downed in one gulp to the toast, *Noroc!* Red and white wines are produced in the country. The best reds come from Murfatlar near Constanţa. The best whites are the dry traminer or riesling or the sweet fete*asca*, all from Cotnari. With their meals many Romanians tend to stick to the whites.

The beer *(bere)* is a light lager. Bottled mineral water, *apa minerale*, is slightly fizzy. Soft drinks are sold straight from the crate at street stalls.

Huber/Schmid

istockphoto.com/Coscubiela

Outside Budapest's most prestigious pastry shop, Café Gerbeaud. | **A luscious display of vegetables in Vienna's Naschmarkt.**

HUNGARIAN WINES

Hungary will keep the most demanding wine-lover in a state of bliss. It's a huge producer of quality wines, though few are household names abroad. The renowned Tokaji (or Tokay) as the jewel in its crown—the wine of kings and the king of wines. Made in the Tokaj region of the Northern Uplands, it uses native Furmint and Hárslevelü grapes and ranges from the pale, dry Tokaji Furmint to the rich amber Tokaji aszú dessert wine. The latter is one of the world's great sweet wines and has had its praises sung by Louis XIV, Beethoven, Schubert and Robert Browning. Its degree of sweetness is expressed in *puttonyos*, numbered from 3 to 6 (the sweetest) and indicating the quantity of baskets (*puttony*) of "noble" grapes added to each barrel of wine. More popularly identified with Hungary is Bull's Blood from around Eger (Egri Bikavér), a red table wine whose name tells you all you need to know about its full-bodied character. It matches with Hungary's abundance of meaty dishes, as do the younger reds, Kékfrankos and Kékoportó, and the fine Villányi-Burgundi. Yet most of the country's wines are white. To accompany Lake Balaton fish, you should try a wine from the Balatonfüred-Csopak Region. From the vineyards around Badacsony, on the north shore, look for a range of white wines using well-known grape varieties, including Olaszrízling, Traminer and Pinot Blanc; red wines from this region are also praised.

Huber/Pavan

Serbia

Serbian cuisine reflects the influence of many cultures: Turkish and Austro-Hungarian dishes feature on the menu alongside traditional local favourites.

Weather permitting, a leisurely meal on one of the many raft or river-boat restaurants at Zemun is a relaxing way to spend an evening. For music in an arty atmosphere, head for Skadarlija.

Pršut (cured ham) and *salama*, a kind of salami, make good starters, as does the winter *pasulj* (bean soup with smoked pork and peppers).

Main dishes are *ćevapčići* (grilled spicy fingers of minced meat), *pljeskavice* (meat patties), *ražnjići* (skewers of grilled meat, optionally served with sauerkraut), *sarma* (stuffed cabbage, vine leaves or peppers), *musaka* (oven-baked layers of minced meat and slices of potato, aubergine or courgettes), *gulaš*, a spicy stew with chunks of beef, onions and paprika, or *bečka šnicla* (Viennese breaded cutlet). A *šopska* or *srpska salata* (salad), sliced tomatoes and onion, sometimes cucumber and peppers, usually accompanies the main dish; out of season it may be pickles of various kinds. If you long for fresh perch from the Danube, then head for the Zemun quarter, known for its good fish restaurants.

If you have a sweet tooth, end your meal with a wedge of baklava, a flaky pastry filled with walnuts and oozing honey. *Palačinke* are pancakes with various fillings such as jam, chopped walnuts and chocolate sauce, or ice-cream. Poppy-seed strudel is another good dessert.

Sremski Karlovci, near Novi Sad, produces the country's best wines. To simplify communication with the waiter, learn the words *bjelo* for white, *crno* for red. The most famous spirits are *šljivovica* and *lozovača*, distilled from plums and grapes respectively.

Slovakia

In Bratislava's restaurants, you might try the local specialities: spicy beef goulash à la Bratislava or fiery shish kebabs with pork, beef and lamb (with ham, sausage, peppers and onions). With them come side dishes of vegetables and various potato concoctions including dumplings. *Loksa* are potato pancakes, often served with roast meats. Smoked cheese is another speciality, fried with ham and served with tartare sauce.

Local wines are mostly white, from the Veltliner, Sylvaner and Riesling grape varieties, and have sonorous names such as *Malokarpatské zlato* ("Gold from the Little Carpathians").

Bulgarian rose *(rosa damascena)*, believed to possess valuable healing qualities.

SHOPPING

There's no lack of opportunities for buying souvenirs of your trip, from Bulgarian rose water to Croatian designer fashions and Romanian lace. Fine crafts are available all along the Danube.

Austria

Not surprisingly, among the great attractions in Vienna—a city pre-occupied by its history—are its antiques. Furniture and objets d'art from all over the old empire have somehow ended up here in the little shops in the Innere Stadt. Still in the realm of the past are the specialist coin-and stamp dealers (where else could you expect to find a wide selection of mint-condition pre-1914 Bosnia-Herzegovina and other imperial issues?).

The national Augarten porcelain workshops still turn out hand-decorated rococo chinaware. Exquisite petitpoint embroidery is available in the form of handbags, cushions and other items with flower, folk and opera motifs. You will find the more elegant shops on the Kärntner-strasse, Graben and Kohlmarkt.

If your taste runs from the exquisite to kitsch, try your luck in the Saturday morning flea market on the Naschmarkt, with plenty of food stalls, too.

Craft products include pottery and jewellery. Small watercolours or copperplate engravings of the local landscape make a charming gift. Dolls in traditional costume are a popular buy, and a good bottle of local wine or apricot schnapps will go down well.

Bulgaria

Souvenirs and handicrafts in the markets, shops and roadside stalls include embroidered table cloths, costume jewellery, lace, dolls in regional folk costume, woven rugs, wooden toys, reproduction icons and paintings, as well as so-called antiques. There are also plenty of serious antique shops around which may hide a treasure or two, but check whether you require an export certificate before buying genuine antiques. You might also like to take home some Bulgarian wine, *rakia* (schnapps) sealed in ceramic urns, rose water, and some of the famous Troyan pottery, especially the casserole dishes which make excellent oven-to-table ware.

Österreich Werbung

Barbara Ender

Konstantin Kovačec

Croatia

The range of crafts is more limited than in neighbouring countries, but you will find wooden toys, lace and embroidery and some attractive jewellery using silver and semi-precious stones. Croatia is clothes-conscious and a few of its designers have made a name for themselves internationally, so you may see something to suit you in the fashion boutiques. And did you know that the form of men's scarf called a cravat took its name from the Croats who wore it while serving as cavalrymen with various European armies over the centuries. Here you can buy the genuine article.

Germany

The shops are enticing, full of quality products beautifully displayed, whether it's food, clothing or the high-tech goods for which Germany is renowned. Toys are among the most attractive buys, from perfect replica trains and cars to charming dolls in regional folk costume. Fine porcelain is another speciality, both in reproductions of 18th-century pieces and in modern designs. Look in the museum shops for superb art books and lithographs.

Sachertorte from Vienna. | Romanian lace. | Petit-point tapestry.

Hungary

Hungarian woodcarving is always popular—especially striking are Hussar chess sets painted in the bright colours of the famous brigade's uniforms. Falk Miksa utca is Budapest's main street for antique shops. Some other good buys include articles crafted from copper, brass or silver; leather goods; handmade carpets and rugs in traditional patterns; embroidered shirts, blouses and table linens. In food markets you will find sachets of ground paprika; spicy dried sausage; a garland of dried cherry peppers; packaged cake or strudel; a bottle of wine or fruit brandy. Music lovers will find a vast selection of CDs: Liszt, Kodály and Bartók, gypsy violins and folk music.

Romania

Traditional crafts continue to be made. Shops called Artizanat sell hand-embroidered table linen, but prices are high. The red woven scarves worn at Orthodox weddings make bright, hard-wearing table runners or curtains. Other interesting buys are brightly painted woodcarvings, reproductions of icons and coloured ceramics.

Orthodox wedding scarf. | Embroidered slippers from Hungary. | Romanian rustic woodcarving.

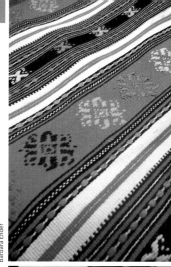

Barbara Ender

istockphoto.com/G. Kenez

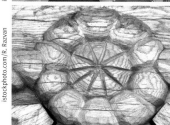

istockphoto.com/R. Razvan

Serbia

Serbian crafts are plentiful and prices are reasonable. Among the most classic buys are embroidery, lace, all kinds of woollens such as sweaters, ponchos, gloves and socks, sometimes quite coarse in texture but incredibly warm. You'll also see sheepskin slippers, as well as ceramics, baskets and woodcarvings of figurines, chess sets, salad servers and so on. Also consider the Turkish legacy: copper coffee pots, filigree jewellery, leather articles — handbags, wallets, belts, jackets and oriental-type slippers.

Try to bargain on the markets. Even in the most serious shops, you may be granted a 10 per cent discount if you pay cash.

Slovakia

For souvenirs look in the shops of Bratislava's Old Quarter selling embroidery and lace, handpainted porcelain, jewellery, wood carvings and fine crystal glass. The word *Starozitnosti* indicates an antique shop, but not everything inside will be old; you may find attractive drawings, watercolours and prints as well as bric-a-brac and assorted junk. A characteristic Slovak craft is wire-smithing, creating decorative objects such as birds, animals or farm carts by shaping wire. Many toys are charming, especially the comical carved wooden animals.

Hungarian Porcelain. Ceramics and porcelain are among the most popular products with visitors to Hungary. Two names in particular stand out. The **Herend** Porcelain Factory is based in the town of Herend near Lake Balaton and has been making exquisite hand-painted vases, dishes, bowls and statuettes since 1826. Herend has proved especially popular with royalty — satisfied customers include Queen Victoria, Kaiser Wilhelm I, the Shah of Iran and Prince Charles. Find out why at the main Herend shop behind Vörösmarty tér on V. József Nádor tér 11.

Zsolnay porcelain from Pécs might not be able to claim as famous a client list, but its products have been far more prominently placed. The company developed a line in brilliant weatherproof ceramic tiles in the late 19th century, and these adorn the outstanding rooftops of Budapest's Matthias Church, the Central Market Hall (Nagy Vasarcsarnok) and the Museum of Applied Arts.

Marguerite Martinoli

THE HARD FACTS

To help you plan your trip, here are some of the practical details you need to know about the lands along the Danube.

Climate

Most of the Danube valley has a continental climate. Winters can be harsh, with occasional snow; in January and February the temperature may drop to −15°C (−9°F). In summer it can climb to 30°C (86°F) or more, and the cities in particular can become very hot and humid, especially in July and August. It is cooler and more pleasant in the mountains or on the Black Sea coast. From April to June, September and early October are likely to be pleasantly warm. Showers are possible, even occasional thunderstorms.

Communications

To make international calls, dial 00, followed by the country code and number, omitting the initial 0. The country code to call Austria is 43, Bulgaria 359, Croatia 385, Germany 49, Hungary 36, Romania 40, Serbia 381, Slovakia 421, Ukraine 380. Internet cafés are to be found in every town and city; larger hotels have business centres with internet access. Many big towns have free WiFi areas.

Customs Controls

When crossing borders between EU and non-EU countries, or between two non-EU countries, passengers over 17 can carry, duty-free, up to 200 cigarettes or 50 cigars or 250 g of tobacco, 1 litre of spirits, 1 l of wine (2 l for some countries), a bottle of perfume. Within the EU, you can pay duty to carry much larger amounts.

Emergencies

All the countries along the Danube have adopted the common European emergency telephone number 112, which also applies to GSM mobile phones. Help from your consulate is only for critical situations and lost passports, not lost cash or tickets.

Essentials

You will need comfortable walking shoes, a sun hat, sun-block and insect repellent. It is worth taking an umbrella. Take light-weight clothes in summer, with a sweater for the cooler evenings. People tend to dress elegantly for the theatre, concerts and the opera.

Etiquette

Old-world courtesies have not been forgotten in central and eastern Europe, where men may still kiss a lady's hand when introduced. If you are invited into someone's home, take a bouquet of flowers and a small gift.

No shorts or miniskirts are allowed for visits of churches or monasteries in Serbia, Bulgaria or Romania. Women are expected to cover their heads, while men should remove their hats.

In Bulgaria, things can be confusing as nodding the head means "no" and shaking it, "yes".

Formalities

You will need a valid passport. No special health certificates are required by European or North American citizens.

Health

There is a reciprocal health care agreement between EU countries from which you can benefit in case of emergency if you carry a European Health Card. Travellers from outside the EU should ensure that they have adequate medical insurance.

Medical services are of a good standard. Many doctors and dentists speak some English. It is advisable to carry supplies of any medications that you require regularly as the same brands may not be available.

Language

Here are some of the key phrases that will be useful to know—and which will be always appreciated by locals:

Bulgarian. *Dobar den* (Good morning/afternoon), *da* (yes), *ne* (no), *molja* (please), *mersi* (thank you).

Croatian. *Dobar dan* (Good morning/afternoon), *da* (yes), *ne* (no), *molim* (please), *hvala* (thanks).

German. *Guten Tag* (Good morning/afternoon), *ja* (yes), *nein* (no), *bitte* (please), *danke* (thank you).

Hungarian. *Szervusz* (hello), *igen* (yes), *nem* (no), *kérem* (please), *köszönöm* (thank you).

Romanian. *Bună ziua* (Good morning/afternoon), *da* (yes), *nu* (no), *vă rog* (please), *mulţumesc* (thank you).

Serbian. *Dobar dan* (Good morning/afternoon), *da* (yes), *ne* (no), *molim lepo* (please), *hvala* (thank you).

Slovak. *Dobrý deň* (Good morning/afternoon), *áno* (yes), *nie* (no), *prosim* (please), *d'akujem* (thank you).

Ukranian. *Vitayu* (hello), *tak* (yes), *ni* (no), *proshu* or *bud' laska* (please), *dyakuyu* (thank you).

Media

The principal foreign newspapers are sold in kiosks on the day of publication. Hotels usually have satellite TV with the main English-language news channels.

Money

Currency in **Austria**, **Germany** and **Slovakia** is the Euro.

In **Bulgaria**, the *Lev* (BGL) is divided into 100 *stotinki*. Coins range from 1 to 50 *stotinki* and 1 *lev*, banknotes from 2 to 100 *leva*. Bulgaria is expected to adopt the Euro in the next few years.

In **Croatia**, the *kuna* (HRK) is divided into 100 *lipa*. Frequently used coins from 1 to 50 *lipa* and 1 to 5 *kuna*, notes from 10 to 200 *kuna*.

In **Hungary**, the *forint* (Ft. or HUF) is issued in coins from 5 to 200 Ft and banknotes from 500 to 20,000 Ft. Hungary is expected to adopt the Euro by 2020.

The currency in **Romania** is the *leu* (plural *lei*), abbreviated RON, divided into 100 *bani*. Frequently used coins range from 5 to 50 *bani*; banknotes from 1 to 100 *lei*. The country is not likely to adopt the Euro before 2020.

In **Serbia**, the currency is the *dinar* (CSD). Coins range from 1 to 20 *dinars*, banknotes from 10 to 5000 *dinars*.

The currency in **Ukraine** is the *hryvnia*, divided into 100 *kopiyok*. Coins from 1 to 50 *kopiyok* and 1 *hryvnia*; banknotes from 1 *hryvnia* to 500 *hryven*.

The major international credit cards are accepted in hotels, restaurants and large shops. US dollars are quite widely accepted, as are euros.

Opening Hours

Banks
Austria. Mon–Fri 8 or 9 a.m.–3 or 3.30 p.m., till 5 p.m. on Thursdays. Small branches may close for lunch from 12.30 to 1.30 p.m.
Bulgaria. Mon–Fri 8.30 a.m.–12.30 p.m. and 1.30–3.30 p.m., Sat 8.30–11.30 a.m.
Croatia. Mon–Fri 7.30 a.m.–7.30 p.m., Sat 7.30 a.m.–noon.
Germany. Mon–Fri 9 or 10 a.m.–12.30 p.m. and 1.30–4 or 5 p.m.
Hungary. Mon–Fri 9 a.m.–2 p.m., Sat 9 a.m.–noon.
Romania. Mon–Fri 9 a.m.–noon and 1–3 p.m.
Serbia. Mon–Fri 8 a.m.–7 p.m., Sat 8 a.m.–3 p.m.
Slovakia. Generally open Mon–Fri 8 a.m.–3 or 5 p.m.
Ukraine. Mon–Fri 9 a.m–1 or 3 p.m.

Post offices
Across the region, post offices generally open Mon–Fri 8 a.m.–6 p.m., and sometimes also Sat 8 or 9 a.m.–noon or 2 p.m. In Austria most close for lunch, from noon to 2 p.m.

Shops
Austria. Generally Mon–Fri 9 a.m.–6 or 6.30 p.m., Sat 9 a.m.–5 p.m. Some have late closing Thurs or Fri to 7.30 p.m.
Bulgaria. Mon–Fri 10 a.m.–8 p.m., Sat 8 a.m.–2 p.m.
Croatia. Mon–Fri 8 a.m.–7 p.m., Sat 8 a.m.–2 p.m.
Germany. Most shops open Mon–Fri 9 or 10 a.m.–7 or 8 p.m.; on Sat shops close earlier.
Hungary. Mon–Fri 10 a.m.– 6 p.m. (Thurs to 8 p.m.), Sat 9 a.m.– 1 p.m., food shops open as early as or 7 a.m.
Romania. Mon–Sat 8 a.m.–8 p.m., Sat 8 a.m.–3 p.m. Food shops open longer (6 a.m.–9 p.m.); some even stay open 24 hours a day.
Serbia. Mon–Fri 8 a.m.–noon and 5–8 p.m., Sat 8 a.m.–3 p.m. The larger shops in cities and tourist areas do not close at midday.
Slovakia. Usually open Mon–Fri 9 a.m.–5 or 6 p.m., Sat 9 a.m.–noon or 1 p.m. Some shops also open on Sunday mornings. Smaller shops close for lunch noon–2 p.m.
Ukraine. Most shops are open Mon–Fri 8 or 9 a.m–7 or 8 p.m, with a lunch break of 1 or 2 hours. Smaller shops close at 5 or 6 p.m.

Public Holidays
Austria

January 1	New Year's Day
January 6	Epiphany
May 1	Labour Day
August 15	Assumption
October 26	National Day
November 1	All Saints
December 8	Immaculate Conception
December 25	Christmas

December 26 St Stephen's Day
Moveable: Easter Monday,
Ascension, Whit Monday,
Corpus Christi

Bulgaria

January 1	New Year's Day
March 3	National Day
May 1	Labour Day
May 6	Army Day
May 24	Culture and Education Day
September 6	Unification Day
September 22	Independence Day
November 1	Enlighteners Day
Dec. 24–26	Christmas

Moveable: Orthodox Good
Friday and Easter Monday

Croatia

January 1	New Year's Day
January 6	Epiphany
May 1	Labour Day
June 22	Anti-Fascism Day
June 25	National Day
August 5	Thanksgiving Day
August 15	Assumption
October 8	Independence Day
November 1	All Saints' Day
December 25	Christmas Day
December 26	St Stephen's Day

Moveable: Easter Monday,
Corpus Christi

Germany (Bavaria)

January 1	New Year's Day
January 6	Epiphany
May 1	Labour Day
August 15	Assumption
October 3	Day of Unity

November 1	All Saints
Dec. 25–26	Christmas

Moveable: Good Friday,
Easter Monday, Ascension,
Whit Monday, Corpus Christi.

Hungary

January 1	New Year's Day
March 15	1848 Revolution Memorial Day
May 1	Labour Day
August 20	National Day (St Stephen's)
October 23	1956 Revolution Memorial Day
November 1	All Saints
Dec. 25–26	Christmas

Moveable: Easter Monday,
Whit Monday

Romania

January 1	New Year's Day
January 2	New Year's Holiday
May 1	Labour Day
August 15	Dormition of the Theotokos
November 30	St Andrew's Day
December 1	National Day
Dec. 25–26	Christmas

Moveable: Orthodox Easter
Monday, Whit Monday

Serbia

January 1	New Year's Day
January 2	New Year's Holiday
January 7	Orthodox Christmas
February 15	Constitution Day
May 1, 2	Labour Days
November 11	Armistice Day
December 25	Christmas Day*

December 26 St Stephen's Day*
Moveable: Orthodox Good
Friday, Orthodox Easter Monday
*observed by Christians

Slovakia

January 1	Foundation Day
January 6	Epiphany
May 1	Labour Day
May 8	Liberation Day
July 5	St Cyril and St Methodius
August 29	Slovak National Uprising
September 1	Constitution Day
September 15	Our Lady of Sorrows
November 1	All Saints Day
November 17	Freedom and Democracy Day
Dec. 24–26	Christmas

Moveable: Good Friday, Easter
Monday

Ukraine

January 1	New Year's Day
January 7	Orthodox Christmas
May 1, 2	Labour Days
May 9	Memorial Day
June 28	Constitution Day
August 24	Independence Day

Moveable: Orthodox Pentecost,
Easter Monday

Public Transport
The big cities are served by networks of buses, trams and metro systems which are reliable and inexpensive. They mostly operate from 4.30 a.m. to midnight. Although more expensive in Germany and Austria, taxis are generally good value elsewhere along your route, and a convenient way to get around the larger cities. Inter-city train services are generally excellent.

Safety
The cities are fairly safe by Western standards. It is nonetheless worth taking some basic precautions. When you go sightseeing, leave your valuables in your hotel or cruise ship safe. Only carry the money you will need for the day along with a credit card. Watch out for pickpockets in tourist areas and on public transport.

Sales tax (VAT)
A tax averaging 20% is imposed on most goods in the EU member states, and in most other European countries. To benefit from a tax refund, look for the "Tax Free for Tourists" sign. The sales assistant will give you a Tax Refund Cheque (TRC). When you leave the last EU country, take the TRC with your purchases, receipts and passport to the Customs desk to get it stamped. There may be a Tax Free booth near the Customs desk where your stamped TRC can be redeemed immediately, or you can mail the papers back to the store in the envelope they will have provided. For more information, see www.global-blue.com.

Time

Austria, Croatia, Germany, Hungary, Serbia, Slovakia: GMT +1 in winter, GMT +2 from end March to end October. Bulgaria, Romania and Ukraine: GMT +2 in winter, GMT +3 in summer.

Tipping

Austria. A service charge is included in restaurant bills, but it is customary to round the bill up by about 10%. You should also leave a small tip in cafés. Tips for taxi drivers are about 10 per cent.

Bulgaria. A tip of around 10 per cent is customary for waiters and taxi drivers.

Croatia. Waiters and taxi drivers are tipped around 10–12 per cent.

Germany. A service charge is usually included. A small extra tip is at your discretion. Taxi fares are rounded up by about 10 per cent.

Hungary. Waiters and taxi drivers expect a tip of 10–15 per cent.

Romania. In restaurants the tip is often included; otherwise it is usual to leave around 10 per cent. Taxi drivers hope for a tip from foreigners.

Serbia. A 10 per cent tip is expected in restaurants and by taxi drivers.

Slovakia. A tip of around 10 per cent is usual in restaurants and for taxi drivers.

Ukraine. Generally a gratuity is included in the bill, but you can leave a small additional tip.

Visitor Passes

The following cities offer convenient visitor passes:

Belgrade: The unique Begrade City Card is a personalised service package conntected through payment card. It offers several discounts.

Bratislava: The City Card offers discounts to museums, on city tours and more, and provides free public transport.

Bucharest: The Bucharest City Card offers discounts to museums, attractions, restaurants and shops.

Budapest: The Budapest Card gives you free access to several museums and attractions as well as to the city's public transport system. It also offers you discounts for some restaurants, shops, spas and guided tours.

Vienna: The *Wien-Karte* offers over 200 reductions on the entrance fee to numerous museums, shops and restaurants, and permits you to travel in the tram, metro or bus for 72 hours.

Voltage

220–240V AC, 50 Hz. Plugs are mainly of the two round pin type. Take an adaptor with you.

Water

Tap water may taste chlorinated, but a wide choice of sparkling and still mineral water is available in shops and restaurants.

On deck in time to capture the Walhalla
monument as the ship floats past.

LANDMARKS AT A GLANCE

The following table lists the landmarks on the left and right banks of the Danube, shown graphically on the fold-out maps "Landmarks left and right".

Legend:
- Castle
- Church
- Monastery
- Ruins
- Archaeological site
- Bridge
- Industry
- Power station
- Lock
- Noteworthy building
- Nature
- **R** Right Bank
- **L** Left Bank

km	Bank	Symbol	Feature	Region	Country
2227		Castle, Church	**Passau**		AT-DE
2203		Lock, Power station	Jochenstein		
2187			Schlögener Schlinge		
2162		Lock, Power station	Aschach		
2147		Lock, Power station	Ottensheim-Wilhering		
2135		Bridge	**Linz**, Nibelungen Bridge		
2120		Lock, Power station	Abwinden-Asten		
2112	**L**		Mauthausen		
	R		Confluence with the Enns		
2095		Lock, Power station	Wallsee-Mitterkirchen		
2084		Noteworthy building	Dornach		
2079	**L**		Grein	A	AT
	R	Ruins	Freyenstein		
2060	**R**	Lock, Power station	Ybbs-Persenbeug		
	L	Castle	Schloss Persenbeug		
2050	**L**		Marbach		
	L	Church	Maria Taferl pilgrimage church	1	
2038		Lock, Power station	Melk		
2036	**R**	Monastery	**Melk**, Melk Abbey		
2032	**R**	Castle	Schönbühel Castle		
2025	**R**	Ruins	Aggstein Castle	2	
2024	**L**	Archaeological site	Willendorf		
2019	**L**		Spitz		

A. Strudengau, narrowing of the Danube Valley

1. Nibelungengau
2. Wachau

Year			Landmark		Region
2019	L	🏛	Hinterhaus Castle	2	
2013	L	⛵	Weissenkirchen		
2009	L		**Dürnstein**		
	L	🏛	Prison of Richard the Lion-Heart		
2002	R	🚢	Göttweig Abbey, 5 km south of the river		
	L		**Krems**		
	L	🏰 ⛪	Gozzoburg, several churches		
1980		🚢 ⊗	Altenwörth	3	
1977	R	❗ ⊗	abandoned nuclear power station of Zwentendorf		
1963	R		Tulln		AT
1949		🚢 ⊗	Greifenstein		
1943	L	🚢	DDSG shipyard Korneuburg		
1939	R	🚢	Klosterneuburg		
1934			**Vienna**		
	R		Danube Canal to Vienna's Innenstadt		
1932	R	❗	Millennium Tower		
1929	L	❗	UNO-City		
1928		⛩	Reichsbrücke		
1921		🚢 ⊗	Wien-Freudenau		
1890	R	⁘	Roman settlement of Carnuntum	4	
1884	R		Hainburg		
	R	🏛	Castle on the Braunsberg		
1880	L		Confluence with the Morava		SK-AT
	L	🏛	Devín Castle		
1870	L	🏰	Bratislava Castle		
1869	L		**Bratislava**		
1866	L		Branch-off Little Danube/Malý Dunaj		
1853	R	🚢	(Lock and) branch-off main arm of Danube and Mosoni Duna	B	SK
		❗	Danubiana Art Museum		
1821			Gabčikovo		
	R	🚢	Lock in Gabčikovo Canal at canal km 10		
1811	L		Confl. Gabčikovo Canal and main Danube branch		
1768	L	❗	Komárno fortress		HU-SK
	R	❗	Komárom fortress		
1766	L		Confluence with the Váh		
1719	L		Stúrovo		

B. Gabčikovo Canal, 38.5 km long
2. Wachau

3. Tulln Basin
4. Danube-Auen National Park

km		Description		Park
1719	🚉	Mária Valéria Bridge		HU-SK
1718	R	**Esztergom**		
	R 🏛	Esztergom Basilica		
1708	L	Confluence with the Ipoly		
1695	R 🏛	**Visegrád**		
	R	Branch-off Szentendre-Danube		
1680	L	**Vác**	5	
1667	R	**Szentendre**		
1663	L 🏛	Church by Imre Makovecz in Göd	C	
1657	R	Southern tip of Szentendre Island		
1655	R ⁂	Roman city of Aquincum		
1648	R 🏛	**Budapest**, Matthias Church		
	L ❗	Parliament Buildings		
1647	🚉	Chain Bridge		
1580	R ⁂	Roman army base of Intercisa		HU
1578	R 🏭	Dunaújváros industrial city		
1531	R	Paks		
1526	R ❗ ☢	Atomic power station Paks		
1516	L	**Kalocsa**, 5 km from the river		
1499	🚉	Motorway bridge		
1497	R	Confluence with the Sió from Balaton	D	
1480	🚉	Rail and road bridge		
1479	L	Baja, port	6	
1447	R	**Mohács**, port		
1433	R	Hungarian-Croatian frontier		
1425	R 🚉	Batina		
	R	Batina-Bezdan road bridge		
1401	L	Apatin	7	
	L ❗	Jelen brewery		
1383	R	Confluence with Drava		
1366	🚉	Road and rail bridge		CR-RS
1333	R	Vukovar, port		
	R ❗	Water Tower		
1299	R	Ilok		
	R 🏛	Franciscan monastery on hilltop		
1298	L	Bačka Palanka	8	

C. Szentendre-Danube
D. Gemenc Nature Reserve
5. Danube Bend

6. Danube-Drava National Park
7. Kopački Rit Nature Reserve
8. Fruška Gora National Park

km			Landmark			
1297		🌉	Road bridge		8	
1255	L		Novi Sad			
1255	R !		Petrovaradin fortress			
1246	R		Sremski Karlovci			
1232		🌉	Motorway bridge			
1214	L		Mouth of the Tisza			
1173	R	🏛	Zemun fortress			
1170	R		Mouth of the Sava			RS
	R		**Belgrade**			
	R !		Fortress in Kalemegdan Park			
1167		🌉	Road and rail bridge			
1116	R		Smederevo, port			
	R !		Fortress			
1113		🌉	Pipeline bridge			
1112		🌉	Road bridge			
1094	R		Kostolac			
1077	R		Ottoman fortress at Ram			
1075	L		Mouth of the Nera River			
1059	R		Veliko Gradište, port			
1048	L		Moldova Veche, port			
1045		🌉	Disused bridge to Moldova Veche island			
1043	R		Golubac, port			
1041	L 🌿		Babakai Rock			
	L	🏛	László fortress			
1039	R	🏛	Golubac fortress	E		
1018	L		Berzasca			RO-RS
1016	L		Drencova, once the end of the Danube cruise			
1011	R ∴		Memorial to Roman emperors, including Tiberius	F	9	
1004	R ∴		Stone Age settlement of Lepenski Vir			
999	R 🌿		Greben Rock			
991	R		Donji Milanovac, port			
	L !		Tricule: two watchtowers in the river			
970	L		Dubova	H	G	
967	L 🏛		Maraconia church			
	L !		Relief of Decebalus	I		
965	R ∴		Tabula Trajana			

E. Golubac Klisura and Ljubkova basin

F. Upper Klisura, former cataracts

G. Lower Klisura, former cataracts

H. Great Kazan, narrows

I. Small Kazan, narrows

9. Đerdap National Park

km			Name		
956	R		Tekija		
954	L		Orșova, port		
	L		St Anna	9	
953	L		Shipyards		
943			Đerdap 1	J	RO-RS
934	R		Kladovo, port		
931	L		Drobeta-Turnu Severin, port		
929	L		Remains of Roman bridge		
863			Đerdap 2		
846	R		Mouth of Timok river		
796			Danube Bridge 2 (Calafat–Vidin), road and rail transport		
795	L		Calafat		
790	R		Vidin, port		
	R		Vidin fortress		
743	R		Lom		
700	R		Kozloduy		
	R		Christo Botev Memorial		
636	R		Mouth of the Iskar		
630	L		Corabia, sugar refinery		
608	R		Somovit, port		RO-BG
597	R		Nikopol, port	K	
	L		Turnu Măgurele, chemical industry		
554	R		Svishtov, southernmost point of the Danube		
537	R		Mouth of the Yàntra		
495	R		Ruse, most important Danube port of Bulgaria		
493	L		Giurgiu, port		
489			Friendship Bridge, for road and rail		
430	L		Oltenița, port		
	L		Shipyards, industry		
385	R		Srebarna Nature Reserve		
376	R		Silistra, port		
371	L		Branch-off of Borcea Branch		
300			Historic road and rail bridge	L	RO
	R		Cernavodă		
	R		Branch-off Danube-Black Sea Canal (Canalul Dunărea-Marea Neagră)		

J. Iron Gate
K. Belene Island,
   former penitentiary

L. Balta Ialomiței
9. Đerdap National Park

261	R ⛪	Orthodox church of Ghindăreşti			
253	R	Hârşova		L	
248	L	Confluence with Borcea Branch			
239	L	Giurgeni			RO
	🌉	Road bridge			
236	R	Branch-off Măcin Branch			
170	L	Brăila		M	
	R	Confluence with Măcin Branch			
155	L	Mouth of Siret (Sereth)			
150	L	Galaţi,			
	L	biggest Danube port for sailing ships			
134	L	Mouth of the Prut			RO-MD
133	L	Border between Moldova and Ukraine			
128	L	Reni, petrol port			
103	R	Isaccea			RO-UA
80	L	Branch-off Chilia Branch			
		= border between Romania and Ukraine			
71	R	Tulcea		10	
63	R	Branch-off Sfântu Gheorghe Branch			RO
0	R	Sulina			
	L 🚨	Lighthouse			

L. Balta Ialomiţei
M. Brăila Pond (Balta Brăilei)

10. Danube Delta Biosphere Reserve

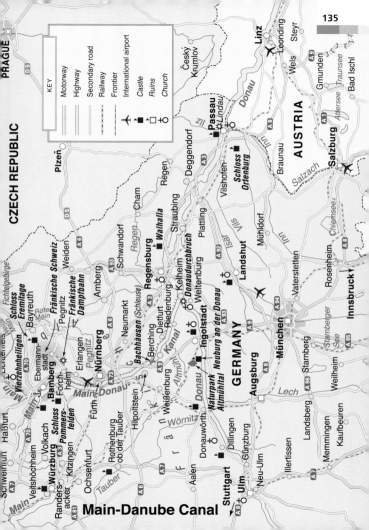

Main-Danube Canal

Bamberg

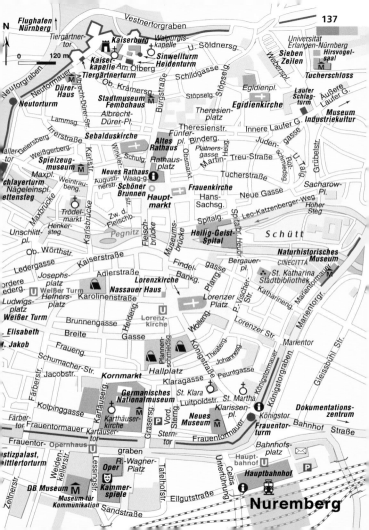

Nuremberg

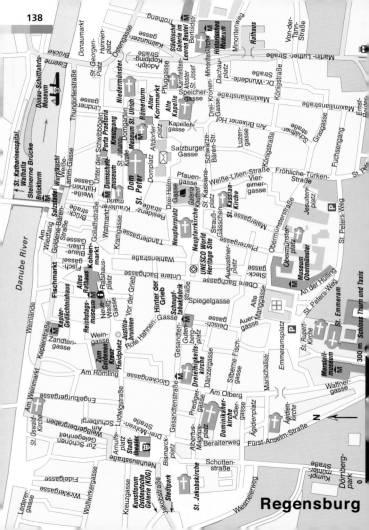

Regensburg

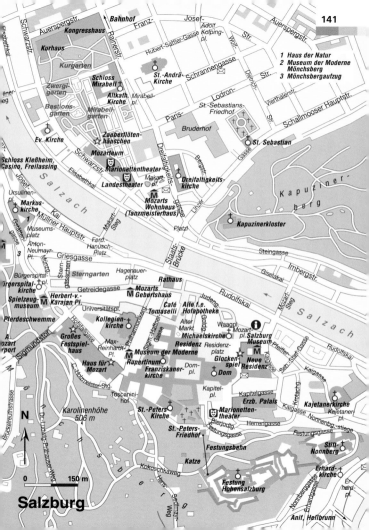

Salzburg

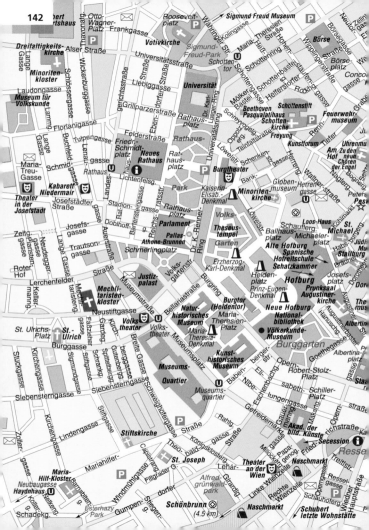

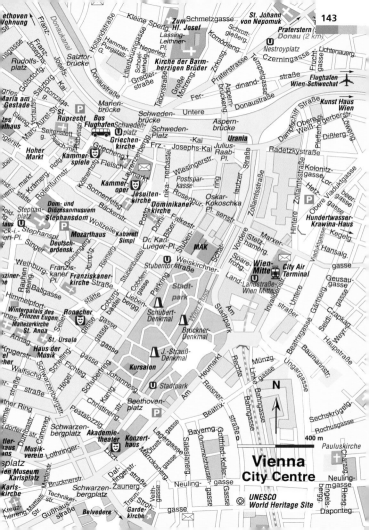

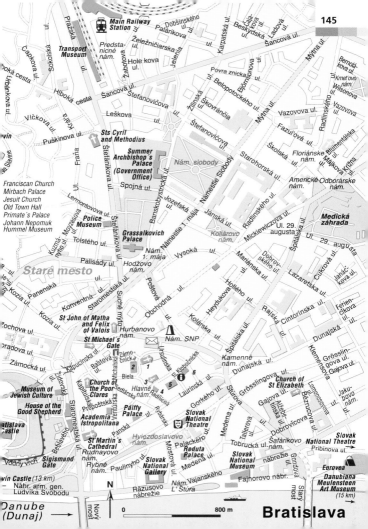

Main Railway Station
Dobšinského
Palárikova
Beskydská ul.
Karpatská ul.
Ladová
Šancová ul.

Transport Museum
Predstaničné nám.
Železničiarska
Jelenia
Hole kova ul.
Zabotova

Bernolákova ul.
Kmeťovo nám.
Wilsonovo

Prašská
Sokolská
Čapkova ul.
Urbánkova ul.

Hlboká cesta
Šancová ul.
Štefanovičova
Leškova
Povra znická ul.
Belopotockého ul.
Blumentál

Mýtna ul.
Vazovova ul.
Radlinského
Vazovo

Vlčkova ul.
Puškinova ul.
Krála
Fraňa

Sts Cyril and Methodius
Štefánikova ul.
Štefanovičova
Zilinská
Skovránčia
Fazuľová ul.
Školská
Florianské nám.
Blumentálska
Májková Krížna

Americké nám.
Odborárske nám.

Summer Archbishop's Palace (Government Office)
Nám. slobody
Starohorská ul.
Staré mesto

Franciscan Church
Mirbach Palace
Jesuit Church
Old Town Hall
Primate's Palace
Johann Nepomuk Hummel Museum

Spojná ul.
Lermontovova ul.
Police Museum
Bankobystrická
Jozefská ul.
Nám. 1. mája
Jánská ul.
Radlinského
Mickiewiczova ul.

Medická záhrada
Ul. 29. augusta

Grassalkovich Palace
Nám. Námestie 1. mája
Kollárovo nám.
Ul. 29. augusta

Kuzmányho ul.
Moyzesova
Tolstého ul.
Vysoká
Mariánska ul.
Dobrovského ul.
Cukrová ul.
Janáčkova ul.

Palisády ul.
Hodžovo nám.
Poštová ul.
Holleho
Lazaretská ul.

Staré mesto
Kozia ul.
Panenská
Konventná ul.
Staromestská
Suché myto
Obchodná ul.
Heydukova ul.
Rajská
Cintorínska ul.
Ferienčíkova ul.
Dunajská

St John of Matha and Felix of Valois
St Michael's Gate
Hurbanovo nám.
Nám. SNP
Kolárska
Špitálska ul.
Grösslingova ul.
Klemensova
Gajova ul.
Grösslingova
Jakubovo nám.

Kapucínska
Baštová
Zámočnícka
Ursulínska
Klobučnícka
Kamenné nám.
Dunajská ul.

Church of the Poor Clares
Michalská
Sedlárska
Biela
Hlavné nám. radničná
Laurinská ul.
Skova
Medena ul.
Gajova ul.
Dobrovičova ul.
Alžbetínska
Lazaretská

Church of St Elizabeth

Museum of Jewish Culture
House of the Good Shepherd
Bratislava Castle
Academia Istropolitana
Pálffy Palace
Panská
Rybárska
Slovak National Theatre
Gorkého ul.
Medena
Tallerova
Dobrovičova ul.
Bezručova ul.

Prepoštská
Kapitulská
Ventúrska
Hviezdoslavovo nám.
Mostová ul.
Palackého ul.
Tobrucká ul.
Šafárikovo nám.

Slovak National Theatre
Pribinova ul.

St Martin's Cathedral
Rudnayovo nám.
Rybné nám.
Paulínyho ul.
Slovak National Gallery
Medená ul.
Reduta Palace
Slovak National Museum
Razusovo nábrežie
Nám. Vajanského
Ľ. Štúra
Fajnorovo nábr.
Gondova
Starý most

Eurovea
Danubiana Meulensteen Art Museum (15 km)

Žižková
Beblavého
Zámocká ul.
Žrídlova
Zámocké schody
Vodný vrch

Bratislava Castle
Sigismund Gate

...vín Castle (13 km)
Náhr. arm. gen. Ľudovíta Svobodu

Danube (Dunaj) →

Nový most

0   800 m

Bratislava

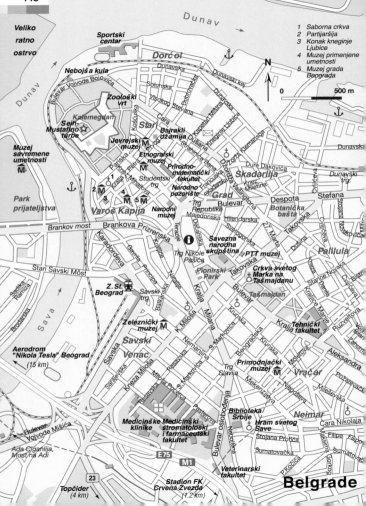

Belgrade

Str. Mihai Eminescu

Mamaia, Delfinariu

Black Sea

Constanța

N

0   200 m

Tulcea/Danube Delta,
Babadag,
Histria,
Bucuresti,
Aeroportul Internațional Mihail
Kogălniceanu Constanța (24 km),
Teatrul Național

Cuza Vodă Str.

Muzeul de Artă

M. Kogălniceanu

Mircea cel Bătrân

Bulevardul

scoala 1907

Bul. Ferdinand

M

Agenția ONT

Str. Dragos Vodă

Str. Tomis

ara Centrala togara IRTA

Primăria Municipiului Constanța

Str. Negru Vodă

Biserica greacă

Str. Karatzali

Plaja Modern

Strada Lebedei

Parcul heologic

Str. Traian

Muzeul de Artă Populară

V. Alecsandri

Bul.

Callatis

Str. Sulmona

Marcus Aurelius

Str. Lebedei

Strada Lebedei

Portul turistic Tomis

Muzeul Marinei Române

Geamia Hunchiar

Str. Tomis

Str. Petru Rareș

Str. Traian

Str. Vasile

Strada

Canarache

Piața

Muzeul de Istorie Nationala și Arheologie

Statuia lui Publius Ovidius Naso

Ovidiu

Str. Revolutiei

Eforie-Nord (15 km) and South (20 km), Neptun (40 km), Mangalia (45 km),

M

Edificiul Roman cu Mozaic

Termele

Parcul Carol I

Romane

Marea Moschee

Str. Dianei

Str. Nicolae

Str. Arhi

9 Mai

Str. Remus Opreanu

Strada Lebedei

Biserica Romano-Catolica Sf. Anton

din 22 Dec.

Str. Cristea Georgescu

Str. Cantacuzino

Ovidiu

Str. Thulescu

episcopiei

Catedrala Ortodoxa Sf. Petru și Pavel

Str. Lumtrei

Str. Grigore Tocilescu

Farul Genovez

Statuia Mihai Eminescu

Muzeul Ion Jalea

M

Bul. Regina Elisabeta

Acvariul

Cazinoul

Gara Maritimă

Strada Termele Romane

Grupul pescarilor

Cruise Terminal

Portul Constanța

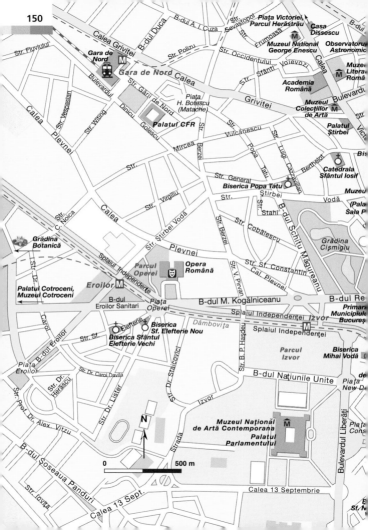

Str. Fluviului
Calea Griviței
B-dul Duca
B-dul A.I. Cuza
Str. Sevastopol
Piața Victoriei, Parcul Herăstrău
Casa Dissescu
B-dul
Str. Frumoasa
Muzeul Național George Enescu
Observatoru Astronomic
Gara de Nord
Str. Polizu
Str. Occidentului
Str. Voievozi
Academia Română
Muze Litera Romă
Gara de Nord Calea
Str. Gării de Nord
Grivitei
Bulevardi
Str. Vespasian
Str. Witing
Dinicu Golescu
Piața H. Botescu (Matache)
Muzeul Colecțiilor de Artă
Palatul CFR
Str. Vulcănescu
Str. Luigi Cazzavillan
Palatul Știrbei
Calea Plevnei
Mircea Berza
Popa Tatu
Str.
Str. Berthelot
Bis
Str. C. Noica
Str. Virgiliu
Calea
Str. General
Biserica Popa Tatu
Știrbei
Catedrala Sfântul Iosif
Str. Berzei
Str. Știrbei Vodă
Str. Stahi
Vodă
Muzeu (Pala Sala P
Grădina Botanică
Splaiul Independenței
Str. Cobălcescu
Str. Sf. Constantin
Grădina Cișmigiu
Calea
Plevnei
Parcul Operei
Opera Română
Str. V. Pârvan
Cal. Plevnei
B-dul Schitu Măgureanu
Palatul Cotroceni, Muzeul Cotroceni
Eroilor
B-dul Eroilor Sanitari
Piața Operei
B-dul M. Kogălniceanu
B-dul Re
Splaiul Independenței
Izvor
Primăr Municipiul Bucureș
Carol
B-dul Eroilor
Str. Sf.
Eleferie
Biserica Sf. Eleferie Nou
Dâmbovița
Splaiul Independenței
Parcul Izvor
Biserica Mihai Vodă
Biserica Sfântul Eleferie Vechi
Str. Dr. Carol Davila
Str. Stăncovici
Str. B.P. Hașdeu
Izvor
Piața New D
Piața Eroilor
Str. Dr. Herăscu
B-dul Națiunile Unite
Piața Cons
Str. Prof. Dr. Alex. Vitzu
Str. Dr. Lister
Strada
Muzeul Național de Artă Contemporana
Palatul Parlamentului
Bulevardul Libertă
B-dul Șoseaua Panduri
N
0   500 m
Str. Iovița
Calea 13 Sept.
Calea 13 Septembrie
Str.
St. N Lo

Bucharest Centre

Aeroportul Băneasa (5.5 km)
Aeroportul Internaţional Henri Coandă (13 km)

Piaţa Romană

Str. Mihai Eminescu

Biblioteca Franceză

Bulevardul Dacia

Piaţa Lahovari

Teatrul Nottara

Piaţa Galaţi

B-dul Dacia

Biserica Anglicană

Verona

Str. Maria Rosetti

Str. Popa Petre

Muzeul Pompierilor

Str. Masaryk

Casa Melik

Muzeul Aman

Biblioteca Centrală Universitară

Biserica Italiană

Piaţa Revoluţiei

Biserica Armenească

B-dul P. Protopopescu

Teatrul Naţional Ion Luca Caragiale

Bulevardul Carol I

Calea Moşilor

Universitate

Universitatea

Str. Plantelor

Palatul Telefoanelor

Bulevardul

Piaţa Republicii

Piaţa Universităţii

Biserica cu Sfânţi

Str. Popa Soare

Muzeul Municipiului

Biserica Coltea

Piaţa Sfânt Stefan

Biserica Rusă

Macca crosse

Bere

Biserica Sfântul Gheorghe-Nou

Piaţa Corneliu Coposcu

Calea Călăraşilor

Biserica Sf. Nicolae

Pasajul Latin

Templul Coral

Biserica Lucaci

Lipscani

Stavropoleos

Biserica Curtea Veche

Sinagoga Mare

Independenţei

Hanul lui Manuc

Parcul Unirii

Piaţa Unirii 2

Muzeul de Istorie al Comunităţilor Evreieşti

Palatul de Justiţie

Tribunalului

Biserica Domniţa Bălaşa

Piaţa Unirii

Piaţa Unirii 1

Unirii

Bulevardul

Unirii

Dâmboviţa

Bulevardul

Unirii

Biblioteca Naţională

Catedrala Patriarhală

Str. Radu Vodă

Biserica Bucur

Mănăstirea Radu Vodă

B-dul Octavian Goga

Central Cemetery

Malashevska
Kozloduska
Grancharska
Kamenodelska
Zavodska
Industralna
Oporska reka
Vladayska reka
Medinkarska
Paulina Unufrieva
Zdarska
Vladayska reka

K. Stoilov
Rodopi
Timok
Dunav
Panagyurishte

bul. Gen. Danail Nikolaev

pl. Stochna Gara

Angista
bul. Vasil Levski
Chumerna
Dunav
1-vi avgust
Sv. sv. Kiril i Metodiy
Simeon
Yosif
11-ti
Ekzarh
Angista

Byalo more
Iskar
Petra
Panayot Volov
Hristo Kovachev
Cher-
nomen
Chatalja
Beli
Dunav
Roatsa
Sv. Paraskeva
Georgi
Georgi
Budapeshta

G.S. Rakovski
Budapeshta
Rodopi
Rila
Veslets
Timok
Kozloduy
Kokotnitsa

Sadchik
Bela
Veslets
Kokotnitsa
Kozloduy

bul. Knyaginya Maria Luiza

Railway Station
Tsentralna Gara
pl. Predgarov

Bratya Miladinovi

Cherni
Iom
Yuri brod
Krusha
planina

bul. Knyaginya Maria Luiza

Radovtsi
Korten
Belasitsa
Struga
Kokotnitsa
Kavala
Ohrid
Strandzha
Vranya

Opalchenska

Ohrid
Sishtov
Karlovo
Kozloduy
Yavorova
chuka
Vranya
bul. Silvnitsa

N. G. Stoilov
Gen. Ivan
Varastsignev
Turgenev
Ivan
Kaliitn
Podpolkovnik

Krasta planina
Osogovo

bul. Silvnitsa

G.S. Rakovski
Bacho Kiro
Pop Bogomil
Veslets
Serdika
Stru-
ma
Knyaginya Maria Luiza

Banya Bashi
Mosque

Shopping
Centre
Sofia
Sinagoga
Ekzarh Yosif

pl.
Lavov Most
Tsvetan
Minkov
Knyaz Boris I
Tsar
Samuil
Listopad

Sv. sv.
Kiril i Metodiy
Stamboliov
Sv. sv. Kiril i Metodiy
Washington
Lozengrad
Simeon
Serdika

bul. Hristo Botev
Kraste
Kozloduy
Krasna
Softroni Vrachanski
Antim
Strandzha
Otets Paisiy

Market
Bratya Miladinovi
Grivitsa
Makaro-
polski
Pordim
Ilarion
Antim
Sveta gora
bul. Hristo Botev
Sv. sv. Kiril i Metodiy
Tsar Simeon
Pirotska
Paisiy
Strandzha
bul. Silvnitsa

Sar planina
Osogovo
Sv. Nikolay
Sofiyski
Opalchenska

Vladayska
Veslets
Listopad
Tsar Samuil
Selon
Struga

Balkan
Chip-
rovtsi
Tsar
Stefan
Simeon
Tony Vrachanski

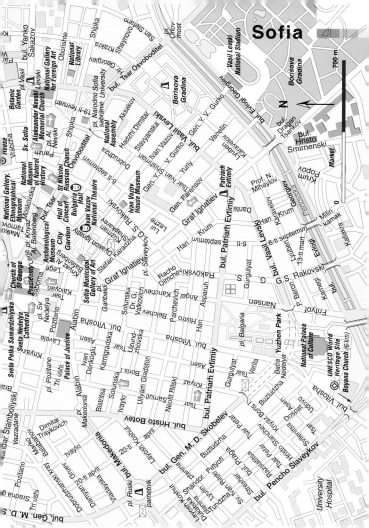

Editors
Eleonora Di Campli
Petronella Greenhalgh

Translation, editorial assistance
Jack Altman

Research, technical assistance
Elke Frey

Design
Karin Palazzolo

Layout
Karin Palazzolo
Matias Jolliet

Photo credits
p. 1 istockphoto.com/porojnicu;
p. 2 istockphoto.com/Stelian, (Danube delta);
corbis.com (pelican)

Maps
JPM Publications,
Mathieu Germay
Jonathan Reymond

Copyright © 2015, 2008
JPM Publications S.A.
12, avenue William-Fraisse,
1006 Lausanne, Switzerland
information@jpmguides.com
http://www.jpmguides.com/

Printed in Germany
12183.00.17324
Edition 2015